£2.50

PERSONS

PERSONS

A Study of
Possible Moral Agents
in the Universe

Roland Puccetti

*Professor of Philosophy at
the University of Singapore*

Macmillan
London · Melbourne · Toronto
1 9 6 8

Published by
MACMILLAN AND CO LTD
Little Essex Street London W C 2
and also at Bombay Calcutta and Madras
Macmillan South Africa (Publishers) Pty Ltd Johannesburg
The Macmillan Company of Australia Pty Ltd Melbourne
The Macmillan Company of Canada Ltd Toronto
St Martin's Press Inc New York

Printed in Great Britain by
ROBERT MACLEHOSE AND CO LTD
The University Press, Glasgow

This book is dedicated
to my early teachers
James Zemek and John Hospers

Contents

Contents

Acknowledgements

THE author is grateful to members of the Malayan-American Commission on Educational Exchange and to the late Professor Lim Tay Boh, former Vice-Chancellor of the University of Singapore, for the opportunity to come to the University as Fulbright Lecturer in Philosophy during the period when most of the writing of this book was done; and to the latter for his invitation to remain there subsequently, in which environment it was possible to see the work completed.

I owe a special debt of gratitude to Professor Antony Flew of Keele University for reading all the chapter drafts quickly and judiciously, and for his many valuable suggestions as to revision. I am also grateful to Dr Robert A. Uphaus of Argonne National Laboratories in Chicago for his painstaking review of the scientific and technical data in chapters 3 and 4. Of course neither of these gentlemen is responsible for whatever faults may have survived their scrutinies.

Mrs J. Wikkramatileke, who typed most of the manuscript under successive revisions, deserves particular thanks for her devotion to this task. Miss Helen Kong was also helpful to me in this regard, and I thank her for it.

A small part of Chapter 1 appeared in the *Australasian Journal of Philosophy* as a paper entitled 'Mr Strawson's Concept of a Person'. Much of Chapter 2 appeared in the *British Journal for the Philosophy of Science*, in a slightly different form, under the title 'On Thinking Machines and Feeling Machines'. I am grateful to the editors and publishers of these journals for permission to use that material here.

ROLAND PUCCETTI
University of Singapore

I *Human Persons*

ANY discussion of persons should begin with human persons, the ones we know best. Whether it has to end there is the subject of this chapter; where it has to end is the subject of this book.

Among philosophers most concerned with the person-concept today, none has made a more original and influential contribution than P.F. Strawson, in his book *Individuals*. Mr Strawson asks why it is that states of consciousness are ascribed to anything at all, and why in fact they are ascribed to the same thing to which we ascribe certain corporeal characteristics, a particular physical situation, and so on. His answer is that these are all ascribed to a 'person', the concept of which is therefore 'logically primitive', or prior to notions either of an individual consciousness or of a body. The concept of a person, he says, is therefore not analysable into a series of conscious states on the one hand or a series of bodily changes on the other. Rather the person is an entity 'such that *both* predicates ascribing states of consciousness *and* predicates ascribing corporeal characteristics, a physical situation, etc. are equally applicable to a single individual of that single type'.[1]

Now while I think this statement is true of human persons, and have no dispute with Strawson's larger purpose of showing how the logical priority of the person-concept can resolve sceptical difficulties arising from the mind-body dichotomy, it would be a mistake to suppose this is an adequate characterisation of our concept of a person.

For one thing, Strawson's characterisation is far *too broad*. This can be seen from looking at the examples he provides of the two kinds of predicates applicable to persons. The first kind he calls

'M-predicates', which are predicates applied to persons and to material bodies as well: that is, to things to which we do not ascribe conscious states. The second kind Strawson calls 'P-predicates', and these include 'all the other predicates we apply to persons', some of which describe behaviour, others less so or not at all. But every P-predicate implies the possession of conscious-ness, even if not ascribing a particular state of consciousness to the subject: this is what marks off P-predicates from M-predicates. Keeping that distinction in mind, the following is a partial list of Strawson's examples:

M	'weighs 10 stone'	P	'is going for a walk'
M	'is in the drawing-room'	P	'is thinking hard'
P	'is smiling'	P	'believes in God'

Now a peculiar consequence of Strawson's analysis may be noted. Of all these examples only the last seems inapplicable in principle to many animals, such as a dog.* Admittedly a dog weighing 10 stone would be a very large one, but we can imagine one stretched out on the drawing-room floor. Dog-lovers, furthermore, will insist that certain expressions or gestures may be taken as the equivalent of 'is smiling'. And if problem-solving is one acceptable use of 'thinking', we can imagine the dog 'thinking hard' about, say, how to get at a bone buried in the garden. If we balk at 'believes in God' (a revealing exception, I think), this does not destroy our case. For Strawson did not claim each example in the list, or something quite like it, must be applicable to anything we would call a person. He claimed only that M-predicates and P-predicates must. And if that were so, then only a primitive Cartesian could deny there are canine persons.

---

* Strawson does not seem entirely unaware of this. In an earlier chapter on 'Bodies' he remarks parenthetically: 'Perhaps we should add "or animals", for perhaps we sometimes refer identifyingly to the particular experiences of animals. But this is a complication I shall neglect.' (Ibid. p. 41)

2

Of course there are people so attached to particular animals that they talk of them and to them as if they were persons. But this doesn't prove much. People sometimes personify familiar *in*animate objects, to whom they never intend the ascription of consciousness, such as a ship or an automobile. And in any case there are fairly crucial contexts, as I hope to show, where no one of sound mind would continue to use person-language with reference to animals. It is in such contexts that we find the distinction between persons and animals which Strawson's analysis glosses over.

But is not Strawson's characterisation of the person-concept also, and in a different way, *too narrow*? For he holds, remember, that a person is an entity to which *both* predicates ascribing corporeal characteristics, a physical situation, etc., *and* predicates ascribing conscious states (or at least implying the possession of consciousness) are properly applied. Thus M-predicates as well as P-predicates must be applicable, in principle, to anything properly called a 'person': which is to say all persons must have bodies. And Strawson leaves no doubt that he means just this. In one place he says: 'a person *necessarily* has corporeal attributes as well as other kinds of attributes'.[2] In another, on the question how many angels can stand on the same pin point, he says: 'If angels are incorporeal and "stand" is given a suitably angelic sense, there is really no limit. But not more than one well-balanced person can stand there.'[3]

Behind this attitude, however, is not an analysis of the person-concept so much as Strawson's 'descriptive metaphysics'. In that undertaking the concept of a person is a 'primary particular' which, like many others, perceptibly occupies space and time and can thus 'be distinguished and identified, as other items having a material place in the spatio-temporal framework can be distinguished and identified'.[4]

Now I mean to pick no quarrel with Strawson's ontology, but if this is really the outcome of conceptual investigation and not just another piece of 'revisionary metaphysics', then surely something has gone wrong here. For there can be little doubt that a great many people speak of at least one person, God, in strictly incorporeal terms. To such people God's incorporeality, far from being a disqualifying handicap, is one of the features of the concept which leads to worshipping Him as 'the Supreme Person'. To them God is specifically, one might say triumphantly, not identifiable in the spatio-temporal framework: for He is thought to 'stand out of', as it were, the world of material objects. They would say Strawson has not shown there is no place for the concept of God in our conceptual scheme, only that there is no place for it in the spatio-temporal scheme: a point they themselves insist upon. It may be that this concept is incoherent in some way, or that one can otherwise show no incorporeal person exists. But Strawson has not done this, and until it is shown to be so one can hardly override the fact that our concept of persons may include God.

To go back now, we have seen ways in which Strawson's characterisation of the person-concept is both too broad and too narrow. What we want to do next is consider how these deficiencies can be remedied, so that we may end up with a characterisation not merely appropriate to human persons, but to all possible persons. Such a characterisation must, for example, exclude dogs, but leave room for God.

As for the first deficiency, it seems we need a third category of predicates, which I shall call 'C-predicates', to suggest consciousness, but not necessarily person-status. M-predicates will then be predicates properly applied to material objects and some conscious entities, including some persons. P-predicates will apply to persons only, while C-predicates apply to all conscious entities, whether persons or not, though never to material objects. One can then reproduce Strawson's list of sample predicates with the following designations:

M 'weighs 10 stone'	C 'is going for a walk'
M 'is in the drawing-room'	(?) C 'is thinking hard'
C 'is smiling'	P 'believes in God'

The advantage of introducing this third category is obvious. The first two predicates on the list apply to material objects, but none of the others. The first five predicates can apply either to a dog or a human being, as we saw, and hence do not *themselves* confer person-status. (I put a question-mark to 'is thinking hard' because whether this is merely a C-predicate or really a P-predicate will depend upon what we mean by 'thinking': a point I shall come back to later on.) But the last predicate is truly a P-predicate, for of any entity to whom it could be properly applied I think we should be willing to say that entity is a 'person'.

The second deficiency in Strawson's characterisation may now be approached along similar lines. Let us simply expand the original list as follows:

M 'weighs 10 stone'	P 'believes in God'
M 'is in the drawing-room'	P 'holds B–R8 an unwise move'
C 'is smiling'	P 'feels a righteous anger'
C 'is going for a walk'	P 'knows the correct answer'
(?) C 'is thinking hard'	P 'is infinitely forgiving'

Here the first two predicates, again, apply to material objects, but none of the others. And the first five, as before, apply equally to a man or a dog (with the same reservation about the fifth predicate). The sixth, seventh, eighth, and ninth predicates could apply to a man too, but not to a dog. Now which apply, if any, to God? Surely not the first two, if He is incorporeal. Nor the next two (except in the figurative language of religious allegory), for the same reason. Nor would the next three predicates, really. If God is omniscient, He need not 'think hard' about something, or 'believe' in His own existence, or 'hold' a certain chess move to be unwise. But the eighth, ninth, and tenth predicates clearly apply: and the tenth to God alone. So that the eighth and ninth predicates are equally applicable to men and God. Interestingly, there is overlapping between three kinds of entities – material objects, dogs, and men – only in the first two predicates. There is overlapping in the possible application of the first five predicates with respect to men and dogs, as we saw. But God never overlaps with material objects or dogs in this list: only with men. Whether this is because 'Man is made in God's image', or because 'Man makes God in his own image' need not concern us here. At least this list of sample predicates shows us how the person-concept excludes dogs and can include God.

We have still not gone very far. The analysis up to this point allows us to amend Strawson's characterisation of the person-concept in a very limited way. We can say a 'person' is an entity such that both predicates ascribing states of consciousness and predicates ascribing corporeal characteristics, a physical situation, etc., *may be* equally applicable to a single individual of that single type; but that the latter kind of predicate may *not* apply to such an entity and the former may apply to entities other than persons. This is hardly helpful.

What is more, even when we turn from these negative amendments to their positive implications we end up with no more than a *circular* characterisation of the person-concept. Consciousness has been represented as marking off certain entities from material objects, but not persons. What marks off persons, I said, not just from material objects, but from other conscious entities, is their quality of being entities to which person-predicates properly apply. And what is that to say, except that persons are persons?

To escape this circle we obviously need to know what persons *are*, and not merely what they are not, or need not be. And I know no other way to determine that than by finding out how we use language related to the concept of a person. Which is to say by looking for common features of person-predicates, and seeing how these combine with *other* predicates when the entity in question is in fact a person. This last clause is particularly important. For the method I have used so far isolates person-predicates in order to bring out their distinctness from either M-predicates or C-predicates. We have seen, for example, that a person need not be such that M-predicates apply to it at all. But it may be that certain C-predicates, correctly so designated because they can be applied to conscious entities other than persons, *must* nevertheless combine with P-predicates if the entity is to qualify for person-status. I shall try to make that stipulation clear as we go along.

But if we are going to look for common features of person-predicates, we need to begin with a much longer list of samples than the last one. And if we are going to watch for possibly essential combinations of P-predicates and C-predicates at the same time, we shall have to include a fair number of the latter as well. The following list, not drawn up in any particular order, may suffice for both these purposes. (For convenience's sake I shall put C-predicates and P-predicates on opposite sides of the page.)

C 'is in pain'	P 'predicts rain soon'
C 'feels hungry'	P 'is a slave to his emotions'
C 'likes warm weather'	P 'considers green an ugly
C 'is looking for a way out'	choice'
C 'dreams continually'	P 'wants to secure justice'
C 'is excited'	P 'is euphoric'
C 'is lustful'	P 'is in anguish'
C 'sees the white box'	P 'appreciates the difficulty'
C 'is sad'	P 'summarised the point
C 'knows the right direction'	neatly'
C 'is angry'	P 'is an astute judge of
C 'hears me coming'	character'
C 'looks contented'	P 'looks at everything
C 'finds it pleasant'	abstractly'
C 'is afraid of you'	P 'endorses your view'

C 'remembers that clearly'	P 'has a pessimistic outlook'
	P 'is absolutely trustworthy'
	P 'refuses to go to extremes'
	P 'is essentially evil'
	P 'detests fuzzy-mindedness'
	P 'has a benign tolerance'
	P 'is absolutely adamant'
	P 'is a smug hypocrite'
	P 'has sybaritic tastes'

One of the first things which strikes me in going through the right-hand column is what might be called the *intellectual* character of many predicates found there. Words like 'predicts', 'considers', 'appreciates', 'summarised', 'judge', 'endorses', 'outlook', 'refuses', and so on: these suggest an 'intellect' manipulating ideas, taking attitudes, making decisions. Undoubtedly it was this feature of the human person which prompted some Greek philosophers to define man as a 'rational being'. Today we would put more emphasis on the fact that humans are symbol-using animals; that they develop in a social environment which includes a conceptual scheme individuals assimilate through learning a natural language; and that it is this, rather than any inherent 'faculty', which underlies their distinctness from other animals. But whatever the genesis of this characteristic, it is there, and it is at least one of the things we find bound up in the very concept of a person.

This brings me back to the reservation I felt earlier about the predicate 'is thinking hard'. As we saw, it could serve as a C-predicate if the entity in question is 'thinking' about no more than, for example, how to get at a bone buried in the garden. But if he is thinking hard about quadratic equations, or the state of the nation, or whether or not God exists, etc., then he is manipulating ideas. The whole process presupposes not only memory, imagination, and intelligence: it also presupposes access to and familiarity with a functioning conceptual scheme. If a dog could do *that* sort of thing, he would also be a person. One of the reasons there are no canine persons, we might say, is just this: that they show no evidence of being able, any more than other animals we know, of really being able to enter our conceptual scheme by learning human language. And this is not just an inability to vocalise our symbols: one has only to look at the sign-language of human deaf-mutes to see how substitute symbols can be found. It is an inability to symbolise at all, without which an entity cannot do many of those things our P-predicates describe.

Another thing which strikes one in going down the list of person-predicates above is the distinctly *moral* character of many of them. Words or phrases like 'secure justice', 'judge of character', 'trustworthy', 'benign tolerance', 'adamant', 'hypocrite', and 'sybaritic' have or easily could have, depending on the context in which they are used, moral signification. They do not occur on the left-hand side of the page at all, precisely because they too are bound up in the very concept of a person. But they do not occur there, not because a dog does not have a 'moral faculty' – no one does, I suppose – but because one of the conditions of ascribing predicates of a moral character to an entity is that this entity be capable of assimilating the conceptual scheme in which moral words and phrases have a natural place. A human infant, for example, is not expected to make moral judgements: but since he can enter the human conceptual scheme he is a developing person and is expected to have a moral character of his own some day. This is never expected of a dog, or at least not in any way which condones the proper application of person-predicates to him.

As I said earlier, there *are* people who use person-language when speaking of or to familiar animals, and often this is moral language. In fact I once knew an American lady in France who kept several fine cats at home, one of which turned psychotic; and this led her to 'pronounce sentence' on the offensive feline as 'thoroughly bad'; she even dug a grave for the animal, made it lie down there, and executed it with a rifle. Such cases are rare, and can certainly be interpreted in non-moral terms. But even if one

9

recognises this feature of human attitudes towards animals, there are, as I said, some 'fairly crucial' contexts in which no one of sound mind would continue to use person-language when speaking of them. And these are often moral contexts. One would not, for instance, speak of 'securing justice' for a dog, because 'justice' presupposes a system of rights commonly recognised by entities capable of conceiving them. We have a society for the prevention of cruelty to animals (by men), but we have no society, and can make no sense of a society, for the prevention of cruelty *between* animals. As R. M. Hare pointed out, it would not be thought oppressive to deny *self-government* to animals, because there is no indication that animals have or could have any desire for political liberty.[5] It is in contexts such as these that person-language breaks down when applied to animals. Which only shows once more, I suppose, the intimate connection between the 'intellectual' and 'moral' character of person-predicates.

But to say there is an 'intimate connection' between person-predicates showing an intellectual character and those showing a moral character is only to say that unless the former can be properly applied to a given entity the latter cannot. Which is to say the former is a necessary, but not strictly a sufficient, condition of the latter. In other words, only a symbol-using entity, or one capable of learning to use symbols, could be the kinds of things correctly described in person-predicates of a moral character. But a symbol-using entity might still be unable to be these things for other reasons. It might be unable to be them because it lacks something *else*, something which the capacity for using symbols and assimilating a conceptual scheme does not entail.

A way of seeing what that 'something' is may be discerned in looking back at our columns of predicates once more. There we note a dog may be 'in pain', but only a person can be 'in anguish'. A dog is 'contented', a person 'euphoric'. A dog is, perhaps, 'lustful'; only a person is properly said to 'have sybaritic tastes'. A dog 'sees the white box'; only a person 'considers green an ugly choice'. Still a person could not be and do all these things unless he were also describable in terms equally applicable to the dog: i.e. as in pain, lustful, contented, seeing something white, and so on. For 'anguish' is logically rooted in the notion of 'pain', even if it is a mental state arising from non-physical causes. This is why it is possible to use 'physical' language to describe such states, as for example in saying 'He found that a painful situation', where you mean 'He was in anguish over the situation'. Similarly, euphoria is rooted in the concept of contentedness or happiness, and sybaritism in (effeminate) lust. Finally, only a person, undoubtedly, has aesthetic reactions to colour, but if he did not perceive colours he could hardly have these. So that many P-predicates *presuppose* the occurrence to their subject of logically related C-predicates as well. In a word, 'persons' are not merely entities to which person-predicates are properly applicable, but also entities which experience in some way those sensations and emotions experienced by conscious entities not having person-status. This is what I hinted at earlier when I said that our concept of a person may be such that C-predicates must 'combine with' P-predicates if the entity is to qualify as a person.

The tie-in with our problem of a moment ago can now be made. Person-predicates of an 'intellectual' character are intimately connected with those having a 'moral' character in the sense that moral-type predicates function only with respect to an entity capable of using symbols and entering a given conceptual scheme. But moral-type predicates may still be inapplicable to such an entity unless the appropriate C-predicates describing sensations and emotions are also applicable to it. In other words, you could have an entity such that its assimilation of a conceptual scheme only misleadingly, if at all, led one to apply moral-type predicates to it. It could act as if, and even say it was, 'in anguish', but because it is not the sort of entity which could be reasonably described as 'in pain', this would be an improper application of the person-predicate 'in anguish'. And the same where X is said to be

'euphoric' without being able to experience a feeling of contentedness, to have 'sybaritic tastes' without ever feeling lust, and to
consider green an 'ugly choice' without really being able to sense
the colour green. That there could be entities of this description
will be apparent in the next chapter. For our present purposes it
will suffice to note a 'person' is an entity to which predicates of
both an intellectual and a moral character typically apply, or
could apply; but that the latter cannot properly apply unless the
entity in question is such that predicates ascribing sensations and
emotions, which are not reserved exclusively for persons, do also
properly apply to that entity in some way.

The phrase 'in some way' will be important to another
consideration I shall take up in just a moment. But before doing
that it may be opportune to introduce now another point
relevant to any adequate characterisation of the person-concept.

What I have in mind is this. We have seen, though only in a
vague and general way so far, how the proper application of
'moral' predicates to an entity is the *sine qua non* of correctly
designating that entity a 'person'. For without giving the point
any concrete illustration yet (which I plan to do in the next
chapter), it has been shown theoretically possible to have an entity
to which intellectual-type predicates apply, but typical moral-type
predicates do not, and that such an entity would not constitute a
'person'. If this reasoning is sound, it seems one can go further
and say, *tout court*, that a person is always a *moral being*, at least
potentially; and that it is the *moral nature*, more than anything else,
of persons which distinguishes them from other conscious
entities. To say this would be in line with my observations above
concerning the breakdown of person-language when applied to
animals in moral contexts. It would also be in line with my point
that proper use of person-predicates having a moral character
presupposes not only the entity's having experience in some way
of related sensations and emotions, but being able to use or learn
to use symbols, and thus entering as well a conceptual scheme in

which moral words and phrases have a natural place. So that to characterise a 'person' as a moral being, essentially, is just convenient shorthand for everything I have argued so far.

The trouble with terms like 'moral being' and 'moral nature' is that they have associations with discredited and really unhelpful concepts in traditional philosophy like 'moral faculty'. Accordingly, I shall abandon these in favour of the less weighted term, *moral agent*. And by 'moral agent' I shall mean an entity which takes, or can take, a 'moral attitude'. That towards which the agent takes such an attitude, in turn, will be a 'moral object'; the agent itself being, of course, a 'moral subject' when taking this attitude. But no one can say in advance what a moral attitude *is*. The actual content of a particular moral attitude is to be discerned by examining properly applicable person-predicates, in their given contexts, which correctly describe that attitude.

There are many moral objects, in this terminology, which are not and could not be moral subjects. A dog, for instance, is or could be a moral object for many human moral agents. Whether or not Rover, for example, should be cared for or put to death, is a moral question which provokes moral attitudes. But Rover is not a moral *subject*. If he bites someone, no one seriously describes this in moral language. To say 'Rover is a mean dog, stay away from him' is not to describe Rover's moral character, but to say what kind of behaviour he exhibits in certain circumstances. No one in his right mind believes Rover takes 'moral attitudes' towards others, then decides to bite some and not others. But since dog-lovers might dispute this, here is a less controversial illustration of my point. For some Hindus all life is sacred. Thus to them a fly becomes a moral object, although in a religious context; but not even the Hindu believes a fly a 'moral subject' in the sense I have given this term. To go on: not all moral objects are moral subjects themselves, yet every moral subject, since it can also be a moral object to other moral subjects, can have reciprocal *moral relations* with other such subjects. It is this dual 'subject-object'

13

feature which characterises what I call 'moral agents'. And I think it will be consistent with everything put forward up to now to say, therefore, that our concept of a person is at the same time the concept of a moral agent. These are, if one likes, the 'moral dimensions' of the person-concept itself.

Nothing of what I have just said, however, should be construed as in any way suggesting that persons, *qua* moral agents, have or must have or should have any *particular* moral attitude towards other persons. R. M. Hare, once more, has shown the fallacy in such reasoning quite clearly.[6] The inference from 'X is a person' to 'I ought to be kind to X', he says, is no better than from 'X is a non-Aryan' to 'I ought to put X in the gas-chamber'. The only way to pass from one to the other, where persons are concerned, is by writing into the notion of a person some moral content of a specific kind. We have to define 'persons' as those entities towards which one should be kind. But nothing in human experience, perhaps unfortunately, has led to our understanding this from the way we actually use words related to the person-concept. There is nothing – and I believe this is what Hare means – in our logical grammar which makes it self-contradictory to say: 'X is a person and I ought, therefore, to be unkind to X.' In other words, though the person-concept involves moral attitudes being taken, and being the object of others' moral attitudes, it is a *morally neutral* concept.

Or is it? One can imagine certain philosophers arguing as follows. They might say that specific moral content *is* to be found in the person-concept, provided we recognise that this concept derives not from ordinary language, but from a Supreme Person's act of will in creating, freely, other persons or moral agents. The difficulties attendant upon maintaining such a view, at least in a way convincing to those who will not accept the premiss unqualifiedly, are too obvious to require discussion here. It is worth mentioning this argument, however, for two reasons. First, we shall have occasion to examine some of its implications in the last chapter of this book; and second, it raises once again the problem of how well my analysis of the person-concept accommodates the notion of a specifically incorporeal person, God.

We saw much earlier that there certainly *are* person-predicates equally applicable to human persons and to God. Both men and God might 'feel a righteous anger' or 'know the correct answer'. But later on I argued that person-predicates having a moral character are not really applicable to a given entity unless that entity not only is capable of using symbols and assimilating a conceptual scheme (as God is, but a dog is not), but also is such that predicates ascribing sensations and emotions properly apply to it 'in some way'. The difficulty here is to understand how an incorporeal being could be such that predicates of this kind could apply to it at all: since many predicates describing sensations and emotions are clearly related to having a body. (The specifically Christian gambit here, that in the person of Jesus of Nazareth God *had* a body, will not go as far as we need. For the very notion of 'Incarnation' presupposes a *prior* incorporeality, and indeed from eternity.) Thus if God would not experience such things as 'pain', 'lust', 'contentedness', or the colour 'green' through a body, how *could* He have notions of 'anguish', 'sybaritic tastes', 'euphoria', the 'ugliness' of green, and so on?

It is not *just* a problem of reconciling the God-concept with our analysis of what constitutes a 'person'. If that were all, one could simply say God is a unique sort of person to whom no C- or M-predicates properly apply, because of His incorporeality, and let it go at that. But in fact this difficulty leads into a very special, indeed crucial, theological problem. For God is conceived as a kind of *super* 'moral agent'. He is represented in one very powerful theological tradition as a moral subject having a particular moral attitude towards all existent moral objects, and demanding from all other moral subjects a similar moral attitude towards Him *qua* moral object. In brief, God is represented as not merely the Supreme Person, but also as a supreme moral *judge*. Thus, even if

He does not experience certain sensations and emotions as arising through a body, He must know what these are. He must know what they are because very often they constitute, or are associated with, human persons' motives or impulses in performing various moral acts and in taking particular moral attitudes. If God is to judge humans morally, it is absolutely essential, then, that He ascertain the specific feelings, sensations, and emotional states of His subsidiary, as it were, moral agents. And to do this, obviously, He must know what they *are*, qualitatively as well as in terms of their occurring to various persons at various times and in various situations.

Associated with this difficulty there is another also inextricably bound up with our notion of God as a supreme moral agent. For part of the concept of God is His perfect goodness. As a perfectly good being, therefore, it is impossible that He should have experienced in Himself those feelings and impulses which, we are told, He condemned as immoral or evil. (Again the Christian may seek a way out by referring to the 'temptations of Jesus'. But, as before, there is an assumption in the Incarnation story of God's prior existence: in fact, without supposing God existed *qua* moral judge before Jesus' appearance, the Incarnation loses all meaning for orthodox Christianity.) Thus God would never have experienced in Himself such feelings as carnal lust, greed, jealousy, sadistic hatred, and so on. And if not, how could He know what they are and be able to judge others' experience of them in moral contexts? Yet as I said He *must* be able to do this. Theologically speaking, the whole concept of the 'Covenant' presupposes His being able to do so. Indeed the doctrines of 'divine retribution' and 'providence' make no sense without it.

The short answer to this difficulty, I suppose, is found in the claim that God is *omniscient*. As such, He would be able to know every event, including all mental events, that occurs in the universe. But as this is perhaps too general, we can reduce it to another more specific claim pretty well universally made by theologians and implied, as well, in much of the unsophisticated religious language of garden-variety believers. This is that God has some unique kind of *direct access* to our mental states. And at first sight this does seem to resolve the whole problem. For as I said earlier, a 'person' must be an entity to which predicates ascribing sensations and emotions are properly applied 'in some way'. The 'way' may now be described so as to satisfy this requirement without supposing God to have a body, or to experience *in Himself* immoral or evil impulses and feelings. For God can, on this argument, have such experiences *as the experience of others* who do have bodies and who do have immoral impulses themselves. To know pain, for example, God need not have pains of His own: it is sufficient that He be aware of, through direct knowledge of my mental states, *my* pains. To know what greed is like, He need not Himself experience greedy impulses: He can know this through access to a human person's state of greed. And the same would hold for *all* sensations and emotions barred to Him as His own experiences by His incorporeal nature and perfect goodness.

But will this really do? Can one by this stratagem make sense of God's being, at least indirectly, the subject of appropriate C-predicates; and thereby satisfying the requirements of a 'person'?

Let us consider what it would be like to have 'direct access' to others' mental states. In order to make sense of this we have to imagine an entity having two distinct *kinds* of experience. An experience X, for example, which is directly known to A as B's experience would have to occur twice (presumably simultaneously): once to B and once to A. If this were not the case A and B would be indistinguishable subjects. But this is not all. Subject A must know X is B's experience, and not his own. Thus A must experience X not simply as X, but as X^b, i.e. as belonging to B. Indeed if this was not so, not only would A not know X has occurred to B, but there would be no way to avoid saying X

occurs to A as his own experience. (And in the case of God this would mean God has a toothache, a feeling of sexual desire, or a sadistic impulse every time any sentient being does.) In a sense, of course, X *is* A's experience. But it is an experience of B's X, i.e. it has attached to it some unmistakable sign of B's ownership. To emphasise this we must say A does not 'experience X', but rather 'X^b'.

So far so good. Now we come to the heart of the problem. If A is indeed God, there will be some experiences arising from having a body and a 'sinful nature' which He will never experience *as His own*. That is to say they will never have occurred to Him as X's, but always and only as X^bs, X^cs, etc. (as the experiences of B, C, D, and so on). But then how will God *recognise* them? It is not enough for God to know that B and C and D are having experiences. He has to know what those experiences *are*. And the only way I can see for an entity to know what another's experiences are, when he has 'direct access' to them, is to have had similar experiences himself with which to compare them. Even between human persons, when there is no question of having direct access to each other's experiences, that is the only basis for understanding, or claiming to understand, what another has experienced. True, we sometimes speak of understanding others' sensations or impulses without having experienced them to the same degree, or in quite the same way. That is often the case with, for example, sexual obsessions or perversions of taste. But to claim this we have to have experienced relevant emotions, etc., to *some* degree and in *some* way. This is why we often say children should not be told about something or be expected to judge it: they haven't had the experience needed to understand it. But the same holds, I believe, equally strongly when it is a question of understanding another's experience to which one has direct access. If God never experienced X Himself, how could He identify X^b?

It seems to me that if one insists God can do this one is

inexorably driven to the position that knowing X^b *involves* knowing X, i.e. entails having X experiences oneself. In which case God *would* have feelings of pain, hatred, lust, and so on every time a sentient being does. But that flatly contradicts the concept of Him as perfectly good. On the other hand, if one insists God does not have such experiences as His own, but only as the experiences of others, it seems impossible to understand how they could have any qualitative meaning for Him: in which case He would be completely cut off from mankind *qua* moral judge. This is the dilemma into which theists are unconsciously led by maintaining God's unfailing knowledge of our mental states; a dilemma which arises, as I said, out of crucial theological considerations, and from which I can see no escape.

I should say at this point that I do not regard the above argument as in any way conclusive. Rather it serves to point up the kind of difficulties one can get into when trying to reconcile an abstract conception like that of God with the fuller analysis of the person-concept sketched out in previous pages. A final assessment of the propriety of including God in the realm of existent persons cannot be made until the end of our journey, after many other considerations have been examined, and will for that reason be deferred until the last chapter of this book. Here we can only say that while Mr Strawson's implied exclusion of God from the realm of possible persons is arbitrary, the postulated existence of such an incorporeal person leaves quite unclear what moral relationships that Person could have with sentient corporeal persons like you and me.

Mention of Strawson's views on this subject brings me to the final matter I want to take up in this chapter. For in fact Strawson allows an exception of a kind to the doctrine that persons must have bodies, when he considers what sense can be given the notion of *dis*embodied human persons.

The reasoning here goes as follows. While the concept of a person is logically prior to that of an individual consciousness, the latter might have a 'logically secondary existence' from having been the ego of a person before the death of his body, and retain its individuality after that as something gained in a previous corporeal state. One can easily conceive this, according to Strawson, in terms of continuing to have thoughts and memories as we do now, and visual and auditory experiences like our present ones. What would be different, of course, is the following. First, we should have no perceptions of bodies we could identify as our 'own'; and, second, no power of initiating changes in the physical world. As a corollary of the first condition, no one else would be observed acting as if he perceived a body 'at the point which one's body would be occupying if one were seeing and hearing in an embodied state *from the point from which one is seeing and hearing in a disembodied state*'.[7] Given these conditions, survival is conceivable, though unenviable. It is unenviable because the disembodied individual is strictly solitary, unable to know even if there are others like him. In order to retain his idea of himself as an individual, he has always to think of himself as a *former* person, i.e. as someone who has become disembodied. Thus he must to a large degree live in that embodied past, in his memories of a prior personal life. There is, however, a kind of vicarious personal existence still open to him: he can continue to take an interest in the human affairs of which he is now only a 'mute and invisible witness'. But as memories fade and this vicarious living palls, the disembodied individual's concept of himself becomes so attenuated that, from the point of view of his survival, there is 'no difference between the continuation of experience and its cessation'.[8] Undoubtedly this is why, Strawson concludes, religious orthodoxy has always insisted on the resurrection of the body.

The first thing to note about this account is its curious overstatement of the consequences of disembodiment. It is not at all clear, for example, why memories of a former embodied existence should fade: particularly when there is no longer a body to become fatigued, injured, diseased, or in any way so altered that memory would be affected by it. (I am assuming no one has shown, really, why memory should weaken with the mere passage of *time*.) Nor is it clear why the kind of vicarious personal existence described by Mr Strawson should simply *pall* after a while. It is true that an *embodied* person would feel frustrated by looking on human scenes he cannot affect in any way: but precisely because he *can* affect them in principle. A disembodied individual, on the other hand, must become reconciled to his status as passive observer. He can hardly have less interest in how the embodied fellows he left behind will work out their destinies than, say, an historian has in the understanding of how certain personages long since dead worked out theirs. Nor, finally, is this prospect of such remote concern to the living as Mr Strawson's tone makes it seem. That some quite recent, familiar 'former persons' should be watching us 'mutely and invisibly' is a disturbing thought: just as it is an encouraging thought, perhaps, that we may ourselves be able to see how those we leave behind will carry on in our absence.

But if the prospect of personal survival is more cheering than he pictures it, the grounds Strawson puts forward to make it plausible are less convincing than they seem. For one thing, we immediately confront the paradox of Strawson's giving 'particularity' to something – an individual consciousness – which by his own ontology should have nothing of the kind, since it occupies no 'material place' in our spatio-temporal framework. But since that is a problem of internal consistency for Strawson, and not for me, I shall let that pass. Growing out of it, however, is a more general difficulty affecting the whole concept of a disembodied yet (in some ways) functioning individual consciousness. This is the problem of how to make sense of such an entity actually 'seeing' and 'hearing' though it occupies no body with a spatial and temporal position.

In one way we can: in the weak sense I think Strawson intends when he says the effort of imagining this is 'not even great'. I am sitting in a chair, say, in a certain room full of people, watching them move and hearing them talk. Now I can imaginatively abstract my body from the sum of things in the room. Neither I nor anyone else sees my body any more, yet I can imagine hearing and seeing everything going on there afterwards. But I am able to do this only by supposing myself to have the same (or some other) temporarily fixed point from which to have continued auditory and visual experiences of the scene. In other words, *as if* I still had a body, though now invisible and inaudible to myself and others.

But of course if I am truly disembodied, this imaginative exercise loses its relevance. For there is no longer any reason to suppose I should have these experiences from the vacated chair, or indeed from any temporarily fixed point in the room at all. The imaginative illusion of sustaining my 'view' of the ongoing scene succeeds only by smuggling in by the back door, as it were, the notion of a particular observational vantage-point gained by a peculiarly ethereal yet spatially located body. It is possession of a body which makes sense of this picture; without it the picture becomes, not impossible, but devoid of any plausibility. Imagine that I were to die in that chair, quietly, of some sort of brain-tumour. At that very instant there ceases to be any good reason why my freed 'individual consciousness' should continue to survey the room's activities from *there*. There is no good reason why it shouldn't happen to find its auditory and visual vantage-point elsewhere in the room. In fact it could find this in the space occupied by someone else's head. Or even under an ashtray, where it can't see anything and hears only muffled sounds.

The situation is really even worse than that. Traditional defenders of the thesis that humans can plausibly survive bodily death have often taken the line that, since 'seeing' does not logically entail 'having eyes', nor 'hearing' having ears, there is no logical obstacle to supposing they do this after disembodiment.

And surely there is not. But there are, certainly, obstacles to believing one sees or hears in a disembodied state more or less *as one did in an embodied state*. One can, again, easily *imagine* doing so, as Strawson asks us to. He says: 'One has simply to think of one-self as having thoughts and memories as at present, visual and auditory experiences largely as at present . . .'9 The question is not whether this can be imagined, but whether one can imagine any good reason, again, for it turning out this way. Suppose, for example, Smith has acute hearing, but is almost blind, while Brown is deaf with perfect eyesight. Now both die. Smith disembodied might suddenly find he is hard of hearing, but sees perfectly; while Brown might find he has, upon death of the body, gained perfect hearing, but become myopic. For that matter, they might now see as poorly as worms, but hear as well as dogs; or, conversely, see like hawks and hear absolutely nothing. The point is simple enough. While one may not need (logically) eyes or ears to see or hear, the continuity and specificity of one's auditory and visual experiences in an embodied state are correlated with having a specific, fairly continuous body; once that is gone all reasonable grounds for expecting the same kinds of experiences, in range and quality, are also gone.

To press the point one step further, loss of a particular body has still another consequence for the individual consciousness. For we can make sense of it as an 'individual' consciousness, as Strawson constantly reminds us, only in terms of it having gained individuality from a previously embodied and personal existence. Without a body it might not only have very different experiences, in range and quality, than heretofore; it might also have no further experience of a relatively stable or continuous kind. The freed 'soul' could just as easily, from a logical point of view, have a perfect *kaleidoscope* of experience, of all kinds and all intensities, and never connected, except in temporal sequence, with anything it experienced before. The chances that disembodied experience would be commensurate with prior experience in an embodied state, therefore, must be very small indeed. No one can calculate these chances statistically, of course. But one can fairly say the logic of the situation makes it highly unlikely that there should be any continuity between an individual's experiences when embodied and when disembodied: so much so that by Strawson's criterion it becomes equally unlikely any sense of continued 'individuality' would be found in 'former persons'. The only kind of 'survival' open to them, on this analysis, would be within the closed circle of memory; and even if this never fades, nothing in the continued existence of such entities could add to the recollection of a former life or make it more interesting, intrinsically, than it really was.

But as Strawson says, religious orthodoxy, i.e. Christian orthodoxy, has always insisted on the resurrection of the body. If this were feasible, some of the difficulties pressed above might dissolve, so it will be worth looking into that possibility.

The most resourceful recent advocate of corporeal resurrection is John Hick. In his essay 'Theology and Verification'[10] Hick suggests deceased humans might take on a 'resurrection body' which is not physically identical with the ante-mortem body (How could it be, if this is now rotting in the ground?), but somehow contains its dispositional characteristics, memory traces, and even the same shape.

The advantages accruing here, by contrast with the Strawson account, are superficially impressive. For by extension from Hick's model, this 'replica' of the original body could have an analogous sensory system allowing for post-mortem auditory and visual experiences continuous with ante-mortem ones: and, if one assumes also a relatively unchanging 'resurrection body', the same stability in experience one had before death. Thus the 'life after death' of the individual would not be limited to recollection of his former embodied existence, but could be enriched by further (and presumably unending) experience in this new life.

But, as one might expect, there is a catch here. For as Hick acknowledges, it would be absurd to suppose the *locus* of such resurrected persons to be just another region of physical space. Nothing rules out that possibility, still to countenance it is to admit, in our space age, the abstract chance that the living might stumble upon the abode of the dead. So one is forced to situate these newly embodied humans in a special 'resurrection world' distinct from physical space anywhere in our universe. This 'resurrection world' occupies *its own space*; in it objects are spatially related to each other, as in our space, but none of them have or could have spatial relations to objects in our world. And in that case it follows that resurrected human persons could not, any more than disembodied individual consciousnesses, be even passive observers of the original scenes they left behind. Which is to say that *all* dead human persons are equally effectively cut off from the living, whether permanently disembodied or resurrected in replica form. On this central point, at any rate, Professor Hick's picture of the after-life is no improvement over Strawson's.

I stress this similarity because of the consequences it has for our analysis of human persons. Hick's account of survival is obviously more appealing on religious grounds. In his 'resurrection world' there is no question of post-mortem *solitude*: one sees 'other members of one's class' all around one; some of these will be former loved ones, and one may be sure those loved ones left behind will follow some day. The *truth* of this picture is, of course, quite another matter. Hick presents it as a logically possible way of achieving 'eschatalogical verification' for Christian theism, so that one can argue for the factual significance of theistic statements. But from this it follows nothing in our this-worldly experience will verify it. Its credibility in this life, then, hinges on a host of theistic assumptions needing independent evaluation (a matter I shall take up in the last chapter of this book). My point here is only that *even if* there was such a 'resurrection world', its inhabitants could have no direct moral relations with the living, and for that reason would not exist for them as full persons, any more than Strawson's disembodied humans could.

What I mean is this. Persons, as remarked earlier, are always – at least potentially – moral agents. This carries with it no implication, as I said, of a particular moral attitude towards other persons. Indeed one can maintain, as Bernard Mayo has,[11] that personal relations are never the same as moral relations. But this is beside the point. The fact is that moral relations, as described earlier, are possible only between persons, and that any entity with which one can conceive having moral relations would be a person. Now what makes the discussion of possible human survival intriguing is not just its conceptual complexity, but the consideration of whether there are or might be deceased humans towards whom one could take some moral attitude. On the popular religious level, this is expressed in statements like: 'I believe Uncle John is watching us now, and that he would want me to do this, not that.' To take *any* moral attitude towards another is to enter into a moral relation with that person, if this is part of the reason for taking it, even when the moral relation amounts to no more than being concerned about how person X judges one's act, and what effect one's act might have on person X. And on this limited meaning, belief in the existence of deceased human persons in another world certainly could affect one's moral conduct in this one, so that a kind of indirect moral relationship is presumed. But that is still a far cry from the sort of relationship between persons where one can, at least in principle, *observe* the effects of one's words or actions on other moral agents. This is just what inhabitants of Hick's 'two worlds' cannot do, and why they could not be full persons for each other until members of the one rejoin the others in that special abode.

Two questions remain, one of which can be answered now. This is the question whether there *can* be (apart from God, about whom there are as we saw special difficulties) persons who are not humans. We can answer this question, I believe, on the basis of the preceding considerations alone. For, as I argued, any entity qualifying as a 'moral agent' would be a person. The proof of this is found, I think, in the observation that to say 'X is a moral agent, but not a person' would be self-contradictory. Yet it will never be self-contradictory to say 'X is a moral agent, but not a human being'. From which it follows that the logic of our language clearly allows for the possible existence of extra-human persons.

The second question, whether or not any extra-human persons actually exist, cannot be answered here. One can only look at the various candidates put forward and decide each case on its own merits. Where a particular entity does not satisfy the standard set above, i.e. does not qualify as a credible 'moral agent', one can reach the appropriate negative conclusion easily enough. But where the entity does meet the standard, nothing in our analysis of the person-concept guarantees its existence. In such cases we can only consider independent evidence relevant to an affirmative claim or, if this is lacking, the coherence of that claim with respect to our general conceptual scheme.

The remainder of this book will be devoted to answering that second question.

1. *Individuals* (Doubleday, 1963 ; Methuen, 1964) p. 102.
2. Ibid. p. 133 (italics mine - RP).
3. Ibid. p. 125.
4. Ibid. p. 132.
5. *Freedom and Reason* (Clarendon Press, Oxford and New York, 1963) pp. 222-3.
6. Ibid. pp. 212-13.
7. Strawson, op. cit. p. 115 (italics mine - RP).

8. Ibid. p. 116.

9. Ibid. p. 115.

10. Reprinted in *The Existence of God*, ed. J. Hick (Collier-Macmillan, 1964) pp. 253–74.

11. *Ethics and the Moral Life* (Macmillan and St Martin's Press, 1958) pp. 194–9.

2 *Person-Artifacts*

WE have seen that while our concept of a person is broader than our concept of a human being, this logical latitude does not itself afford the basis for an inference to the existence of extra-human persons. Such an inference requires, as I said, two things. First, we must satisfy ourselves that the entity in question meets conceptual standards for person-status; and second, we must consider the relevant evidence for its existence or, where this is indecisive, its coherence with respect to our general conceptual scheme.

In this chapter I shall be examining the notion of two entities with this in common: that if they existed and qualified as persons they would be *artificial* persons. But in neither case will existential questions arise, for one of these entities does not so far as we know exist anywhere and is not likely to exist for a long time; whereas the other certainly does exist, at least in prototype form, and no one will dispute that. The latter, which I shall discuss first and at greater length in this chapter, raises a problem only about whether at present or in future refined versions it does or could come to meet our conceptual requirements for person-status.

The claim that computer-based machines might achieve person-status is rooted pretty firmly in the sub-claim that such machines are indeed 'thinking' entities. As we saw in the preceding chapter, 'thinking' certainly is implied in the content of many typical 'P-predicates': so much so that one of the essential ingredients of the person-concept is, I argued, that of an 'intellect' at work. There were, however, some important qualifications made in this connection, and I shall have occasion to bring them to bear on our present topic as we go along. Let us first see how much can be said for this initial claim that some machines do think.

At the very beginning of our consideration we confront the logical obstacle that our language imposes, namely that as we now use words related to the concept 'thinking' it would be strange to say of any inanimate thing that it 'thinks'. As we saw earlier, there is no difficulty in saying this of many animals, such as a dog, where the kind of 'thinking' ascribed amounts to no more than simple problem-solving. Yet even those technically familiar with the most advanced computer machines, which are capable of very intricate problem-solving indeed, are commonly reluctant to apply this predicate to them. Thus philosophers are tempted to take the short way with this issue and say machines cannot think because we cannot properly *say* they do: ordinary usage will not permit it. So we have to stop and ask, first of all, if machines *can be said* to think.

Certainly the question 'Do machines think?' is not a straightforward empirical one like 'Do Hottentots ever cry?', which we could settle by making the appropriate observations. If it were, we might get the answer from machine technicians: whereas these people, as I said, do not themselves know how to answer. Rather it is a question like 'Do cats fall in love?', where the answer depends to a great extent on agreeing to accommodate, or not to accommodate, the known facts to an established conceptual scheme. But if our question is linguistic in this sense, rather than factual, that does not mean we are bound to answer it strictly in accord with current usage. As Hilary Putnam observed,[1] some linguistic issues need to be studied 'diachronically' rather than 'synchronically'. This is so not because the concepts at stake are changing, but because technological and scientific advances often provide new contexts for old concepts. To use his example, the Greek equivalent of 'I am a thousand miles from you' could hardly have had a standard use (in inter-personal address) before the invention of writing. After that it *acquired* a standard use without changing the meaning of any of the words. A formerly 'deviant'

Greek sentence then became 'non-deviant' or normal. So our question is not really whether machines can be said to think in terms of contemporary usage. It is whether the paradigm sentence, 'This machine is thinking' could acquire a standard English use in future. Is it feasible, in other words, that extension of our present machine technology could provide contexts in which that sentence would be non-deviant?

I think it pretty clearly could. Consider the following imaginative, but not wholly implausible, extension of current technological capabilities. Imagine an automobile exactly like those we know except that it contains within it a mechanical unit physically analogous to contemporary computing machines. The addition of this unit does not alter our concept of the entity as an automobile, any more than installation of a radio, telephone, or air-conditioning system does. But it will make a striking difference in its performatory characteristics, because with this unit the vehicle now becomes *self-directing* (for this reason I shall call the unit 'SDAD', for 'Self-Directing Automatic Driver'). We shall locate our SDAD unit in the space normally occupied by the driver, with suitable attachments to ignition, accelerator, brakes, gears, clutch, horn, steering-wheel, and light switches. Its memory banks include a complete model of the city's streets, with all the necessary data for appropriate actuations in order to get the automobile from its present *locus* to any place corresponding to a point on the model. The stimulus for its operation may be a simple push on a button indicating where the owner of the car wants to go, but more sophisticated versions may respond to a verbal order such as 'Sixteenth and Vine streets, please!' SDAD'S programming will include all normal responses to driving situations in a modern city: for example, slowing down when approaching a vehicle going in the same direction and passing on one side only, provided no vehicle is coming from the opposite direction in the same lane. Its photo-electric sensors will allow the car to respond to conventional traffic signals of a mechanical or electrical kind, to come to a complete stop if a large object or hole appears ahead, etc. Re-programming is necessary only when signals are changed or new streets opened.

This is already an impressive machine, but we can still improve on it. Imagine now the installation of a more advanced unit, which I shall call 'Super-SDAD'. The distinctive feature of Super-SDAD is that it has 'higher-order programming', i.e. it modifies its own basic programme in accordance with the results obtained so as to find better ways of achieving its overall goals. Thus an automobile equipped with Super-SDAD is not only self-directing: it learns from experience and is able to solve unforeseen problems (whether we mean by 'it' the unit itself or the automobile as a whole does not matter for our purposes). To get to our problem now, suppose the owner and a passenger are in the back of a Super-SDAD car. The owner says into the speaker: 'Sixteenth and Vine streets, please!' They sit back and relax. But at the corner of Fourth and Vine the car comes to a slow stop. The passenger asks, 'What's the matter? Isn't it working? Why doesn't it go on?' The owner replies: 'Wait a minute. *It's thinking.*' After a brief period the automobile changes gear, turns to the left, and proceeds up Fourth Street in a northerly direction. 'You see', comments the owner, 'it's going to try another route to escape that heavy downtown traffic.' I do not believe anyone can fairly say the situation just described is technologically *impossible*, however fanciful it may appear. And if not, it is easy to see how the sentence 'This machine is thinking' *could* acquire a standard use; so that there is after all no fundamental conceptual incongruity in the claim we are considering.

Note that nothing in the above picture involves the ascription of *conscious states* to the machine. 'Thinking' is attributed to the machine in a perfectly neutral way, so far as consciousness is concerned; as no more, in fact, than a predicate describing what the machine was *doing* when it paused at Fourth and Vine streets. What it did, of course, is the following things: (1) scanned its memory store for experiences of route conditions at that time and in that place; (2) recollected that here traffic becomes heavy; (3) reviewed its program for alternative routes to the same destination; (4) selected one of these in a scientifically unpredictable fashion; and (5) proceeded on the new route in accordance with its overall goal of getting from one point to another as quickly and safely as possible. Now if one says consciousness is inseparable from such refined ratiocinative operations, it follows the machine was conscious when doing these things. If one says, on the other hand, that machines are never conscious, it follows that ratiocinative thinking need not be accompanied by conscious states. What does *not* follow from a denial of consciousness is that the machine was not thinking. For if the above operations are not instances of thinking, then what are they instances of? It seems clear we have no word that is not a synonym of 'thinking' to describe them. One could of course invent another word, but if I am right about this that new word would also serve to describe what a human driver does in the same situation: it would be still another synonym for 'thinking'. To say this is not to endorse behaviourism in general; it is only to point out that one perfectly legitimate use of 'thinking' is merely descriptive of ratiocinative processes and therefore independent of talk about conscious states.

We are now in a position to see how the proliferation of computer-based machines with higher-order programming might lead to applying many rather typical P-predicates to them. Look for example at the following list of sample P-predicates taken from the previous chapter.

P 'holds B–R8 an unwise move'	P 'looks at everything abstractly'
P 'knows the correct answer'	P 'endorses your view'
P 'predicts rain soon'	P 'is absolutely trustworthy'
P 'appreciates the difficulty'	P 'refuses to go to extremes'
P 'summarised the point neatly'	P 'detests fuzzy-mindedness'

I believe every one of these predicates could, given a suitable context, have a proper application to such machines. Indeed the first three in the list pretty obviously apply to some of the better-known existing machines. But since this is an important aspect of the larger claim we are considering – namely the right of such entities to person-status – it will be worth while considering how that is so in each instance. What follows is a series of contexts suitable to the application of each sample predicate.

1. We have a machine programmed to play chess, in which all the basic rules of the game are inviolable and its overall goal is to bring the opponent's King into checkmate before he can do the same. With sufficient experience against good players, the machine learns to avoid certain situations, pursue certain combinations, and so on. It is just as difficult to predict which move the machine will make in a particular board position as it is to predict a human player's move. Now the machine faces a situation where to some observers B–R8 seems the obvious reply. The machine hesitates, however, and tries Q Kt–K2: not so obvious, but perhaps less risky. What would be strange or absurd about saying 'It holds B–R8 an unwise move'?

2. Two mathematicians are trying to work out the implications of a certain equation. To save time they run it through a computer, get an answer, and check this out successfully. What is wrong with one saying to the other 'It knows the correct answer'?

3. A computer is programmed to make meteorological predictions: not the way barometers do, but the way meteorologists do. All the relevant data are fed into the machine, which correlates these with similar data from its memory store, then 'predicts rain soon'.

4. In a given problem, say in games theory, some machines have had bad results through overriding a concealed complication. The present machine stops at that point and works it out carefully before proceeding further. It seems perfectly natural to

say of this machine that, in contrast to the others, it 'appreciates the difficulty'.

5. A computer has been programmed to make quick and comprehensive surveys of legal precedents on any of several points of law. A particularly complex task of this sort is set the machine, and the results are presented to an expert in the subject, who then says: 'Yes, it summarised the point neatly.'

6. Several higher-programmed machines are employed in the study of historical situations: the aim being to see if, on the given data for a certain period, they can predict subsequent historical developments and therby test the relative importance of diverse factors in those periods. Of one of these machines it is noted that its particular approach to the data is characterised by the fact that it tends to 'look at everything abstractly' rather than 'concretely'.

7. A computer is programmed to make speedy diagnoses of various illnesses. This it does exactly the way a doctor does, except that its memory store of symptoms is larger and its ability to correlate these with specific illnesses surer. In a particularly difficult case where two diagnosticians are in disagreement the relevant data are fed to the machine and a diagnosis obtained. Holding up the slip of paper, one says to the other: 'It endorses your view.'

8. One computer in a laboratory is seen to be erratic in its performance, sometimes getting good results, sometimes getting very wild answers. By way of contrast a technician points to another and says: 'It's absolutely trustworthy.'

9. Again comparing computers, programmed this time to play chess with each other, it is noted that computer A takes great risks in difficult situations, sometimes with brilliant results, often leading to sure defeat. Computer B, on the other hand, characteristically chooses a more conservative, but in the long run sounder, line of play. We might very well say of B, by contrast to A, that it 'refuses to go to extremes' in the game.

10. A given machine with higher-order programming simply

35

will not work with signals imprecisely defined, whereas others will. Of it someone says, and is well understood in the context, that the machine 'detests fuzzy-mindedness'.

Now if these are perfectly feasible ways of describing some machines, either existing ones or extensions of them in the not too distant future, it follows that at least 'intellectual-type' P-predicates overlap in possible application to men and machines. Philosophers hostile to this inference may, however, resist it on these grounds. They may say that even if, as I argued, 'thinking' can refer to ratiocinative processes without necessarily imputing consciousness to the entity in question, still the application of these sample predicates to men involves in each case the ascription of conscious states. (A probable exception is the eighth predicate in our list, which can describe unthinking entities too.) Thus there cannot be a real parity of application unless we are willing to ascribe consciousness to machines: which is supposed to be self-evidently absurd. But the only basis I can find for this view takes the form of assuming that consciousness accompanies ratiocinative processes only in *living* things; so that machines are never conscious precisely because they are *not enough like us*. As I hope to show later on, there *is* a way in which this point becomes crucial to the larger claim we are considering, but in the present connection it strikes me as completely unwarranted. I am not saying these machines are conscious when thinking: I do not see how we could know that one way or the other. But I am saying this argument rests on a premiss which is itself hopelessly provincial. For on that premiss, I submit, a conscious thinking machine might use exactly the same argument to show humans do not think.[2]

Thus we come face to face with the question whether in fact *all* P-predicates might not be applicable to machines as well as to men, so that some machines might eventually qualify as persons.

The best way to approach this question, I believe, is in terms of the conventional spectre of humanoid or parahuman robots.

Suppose we imagine a group of computer scientists and assorted technicians resolved to play an elaborate joke on an exceptionally timid friend named Simon. In their spare time and in great secrecy they construct a mannequin of a beautiful young woman, complete with the usual feminine accessories. It has mechanical sensors connected with the mannequin's external 'sense-organs', a simulated respiratory cycle, heart-beats and pulse-beats, a special voice-production box, and so on. The head cavity contains a condensed digital computer with a storage capacity of 10^7 binary digits. Its program controls the above functions of the mannequin realistically and includes a fairly large set of stock replies to stock questions. When the machine's interlocutor is identified as Simon, it actuates another, unusually warm set of responses. We now have a full-fledged lady robot. They give her the name 'R. Sally I'.

Our conspirators next arrange a special cocktail party, in the course of which shy Simon meets Sally for the first time. Her deference and eagerness towards him produce the expected result. After the party he goes about asking people who she is and trying to arrange further meetings with her. This success emboldens Simon's friends. They rehaul Sally and give her not only a larger storage capacity, but a randomising circuit feature which will enable her to learn from experience with Simon and adjust her future responses to unforeseen situations. The new program also includes tactual reactions of a well-defined kind. Re-named 'R. Sally II', the mannequin is then placed in a *boudoir* situation and an assignation with Simon arranged. To everyone's delight the deception is again successful: Simon prevails.

But now a strange thing happens. Simon falls in love; he even talks of marriage in the spring. The conspirators become alarmed. What should they do? Should they tell him the truth before it is too late? But what if he commits suicide? On the other hand, suppose he does marry her. If he never finds out, what harm will have been done? After all, Sally *is* learning. If she becomes difficult they can always change her program again. At this point, however, fate intervenes. Sally slips in the bathtub and fractures her skull. Simon finds her lying inert on the bathroom floor, broken transistors all about: the truth is out.

Let us imagine two quite distinct reactions to this. In Reaction A Simon goes to his friends and says: 'I forgive you for what you did, but you must help me now. I don't care if Sally was a machine. I was never so happy as when I had her. Please, please *put her back together again*!' We can imagine Simon's friends being sympathetic to this plea. They might also be repulsed by it, since it hardly seems healthy to want to continue a love affair with a machine, even one so accommodatingly programmed as Sally. But this is a psychological repulsion, not a moral one: or at least not obviously moral. For no one in this situation, not even Simon, believes Sally is a moral object. They do not believe this because they do not believe Sally has feelings. Thus it would not matter to them, except for what effect it might have on his own status as a moral subject, what Simon does with a reconstructed R. Sally II. Even if Simon were a secret sadist this would not matter; there can be no moral relationship between him and Sally if she cannot be hurt, either physically or emotionally. She can only *seem* to be hurt, on this interpretation. If Simon wants to live with an illusion, that could be of moral concern only with respect to the possible consequences this might have on his relations with other people.

But suppose Simon has a different, in some ways stronger, reaction. In Reaction B he goes to his friends and says: 'I forgive you for what you did, but you must help Sally now. She was a fine and sensitive girl, so much in love with life! Restore her happiness with me: please, please put her back together again!' In this case Simon's friends might attempt to persuade him he has the whole thing wrong. They might point out that they *made* Sally what she seemed to be. But what can they say that would be absolutely convincing on this score? Suppose they say: 'Look here, Simon, she didn't really love you, or get pleasure from your embraces.

We only programmed her to *act* that way, though in her later form she was able to review and modify that program. We could make her tomorrow with a different program, so that every time you touch her she'll scream in agony. Don't you see she's just an intelligent doll?' Simon can still answer: 'Oh, don't do that. Don't cause her any pain. Remake her just the way she was before, so she can be happy with me as she used to be.' Or suppose they dissect Sally before his eyes, alongside a human cadaver, and show him how very different are the materials of which she is constructed. Could he not maintain that in spite of these differences Sally's structure and functions give rise to sensations and emotional states? What can Simon's friends do to prove he is wrong? Indeed, is there any way of showing conclusively that a highly adaptable lady robot like Sally does *not* have feelings when her performance is parahuman?

Some recent writers on this subject have argued forcibly that there is not. To take an example, Professor Michael Scriven[3] says the view that because a machine is designed to say it is in love it cannot really be in love is false, 'for the design may, and perhaps must, achieve both ends'. Performatory evidence for feelings is not decisive, he admits, but it fulfils a 'necessary condition' of supposing them to occur. And what would be a sufficient condition? 'The answer must be that there is no *logically* sufficient condition statable in terms that can be verified by an external observer.' Thus if a computer-based system reports consciousness of pain, this may be accepted as true under certain conditions. The essential condition is that the machine be taught the language of feelings 'with great care', so that it possesses and knows to be relevant 'every statable proposition' involving sensations and emotions. Once this is achieved, it would be 'wholly unreasonable', Scriven claims, to deny that it has feelings.

Professor D. M. MacKay[4] has illustrated the analogical strength of arguments like this by means of a very suggestive 'semantic chart'. It is reproduced here in its entirety:

D   39

NATURAL		ARTIFICIAL	
Personal aspect	Mechanical aspect	Mechanical aspect	Personal aspect
	Growth	*Construction*	
Person	*Brain-and-Body*	*Automation*	?
(Joe)	('Mass of *cells* & things')	('Mass of *wires* & valves')	?
	Carrying *signals*	Carrying *signals*	
	Forming an *information-system*	Forming an *information-system*	
	Organising observable *behaviour*	Organising observable *behaviour*	
	indicative of	*indicative* of	
Thinks, feels, hopes, fears . .	Thinking, feeling, hoping, fearing . . .	Thinking, feeling, hoping, fearing . . .	

What MacKay wants to suggest, of course, is that when the analogy between the two inner columns is strong enough, it cannot be absurd in all circumstances to pass from the inner to the outer column on the right-hand side just as we do on the left-hand side. All that is required, says MacKay, is a 'commitment' to use personal language towards the artificial entity as one does towards natural entities. Presumably there is no bar to doing this in the fact that natural and artificial entities have distinct origins and structural components.

What seems to underlie the stand of Scriven and MacKay on this, as I suppose it underlies the opposite stand of more conservative philosophers, is what might be called the presupposition of a unitary mental life. The human being reasons, calculates, predicts, etc., consciously. The human being also sees, hears, hopes, despairs, feels pain or pleasure, etc.: all of which involve conscious states. Now one can certainly make out a strong case for machines performing these ratiocinative operations in a parahuman way, and as I said before there seems to be no good reason whatever for insisting that machines are not conscious when doing so. If so, the natural response will be to go one step further and attribute feelings to machines when they are able to behave *as if* they see, hear, hope, despair, feel pain or pleasure. Those who take a position like Scriven's and MacKay's know perfectly well, of course, that such behaviour cannot establish the existence of feelings in machines. But they hasten to point out that nothing in the behaviour of any human other than oneself does this either. Their view on this, in other words, is that we have before us an all-or-nothing proposition; that no logical wedge can be driven between thinking and feeling; and that one must therefore either deny or accept both. MacKay's chart pretty clearly reveals this at the bottom of the inner columns, where behaviour patterns indicative of 'thinking, feeling, hoping, fearing' are all lumped together.

It will be convenient to recall in this connection a point made in the previous chapter. There I remarked that analysis of the concept of a person requires not merely looking for common features of typical P-predicates, but also seeing how these combine with C-predicates when the entity in question is in fact a person. For many P-predicates, as I said, presuppose the occurrence to their subject of logically related C-predicates. Thus the *proper* application of P-predicates often depends on whether or not certain C-predicates really have a proper application to the same entity. This is particularly the case, I argued, with 'moral-type' P-predicates: so essential to our concept of a person. One of the conditions of applying these to a machine is satisfied, or would be satisfied, by the machine's being able to enter into or assimilate our conceptual scheme. For, as I maintained in that chapter, moral-type P-predicates have application only to an entity able to do this. But again we must recognise that one could have an entity such that its assimilation of our conceptual scheme only misleadingly encourages us to apply these predicates to it. It could act as if, or even say it is, disappointed or in love or anguishing; but because it is not the sort of entity to which requisite sensations and emotional states can be creditably applied, such descriptions would be improper. The crux of our problem, then, is whether the assimilation of human language by a machine would carry with it the implication of feeling-occurrences.

How we shall answer this depends quite heavily on what we understand by Scriven's important stipulation of 'teaching a machine the language of feelings'. I have no doubt a machine could learn to use words referring to sensations and emotional states, as alternative ways of describing its internal changes. It may discover, for example, that 'I have a pain in my left shoulder' will do just as well as 'R. Sally II has an overload current at LX5612'; or that 'I'm getting bloody annoyed' will serve to express 'Pre-set goal Z cannot be attained under present conditions'. And this is surely *one* acceptable meaning of 'learning the language of feelings'. But it is not the only one. As has been pointed out by others,[5] a blind man may know 'the grass is green' without knowing what is *meant* by saying this. Leaving that aside, however, it is quite another matter to claim that the machine's having learned to say this makes it 'wholly unreasonable' to deny it has feelings of pain or anger. After all, the human infant *first* experiences pain, anger, etc., and then gradually finds the words used in a public language to describe them. The feelings do not arise from learning to use these words, but in the experience of the organism referred to by them. So that before one can accept learning the language of feelings as a reasonable proof of the occurrence of feeling-states one has to assume what Scriven's argument is intended to show: that the machine does have feelings.

To get back to MacKay's chart now, it is easy to see how philosophical conservatives get off on the wrong foot in resisting such imputations. They tend to argue that because of what appears at the top of the inner columns there the analogy in the outer columns can never be justified. I think this is a mistake if one means nothing 'constructed', rather than 'grown', could conceivably have feelings. (Indeed I shall attempt to show the contrary later on in this chapter.) But where they seem on the right track is in the suspicion that nothing *inorganic* could have, not conscious ratiocinative processes, but sensations, emotional states, etc. The fatal flaw in MacKay's chart occurs, I believe, not at the very top of the inner columns, so much as in the third line. In other words, it is a difference of *components*, rather than origins, which vitiates his analogy in the outer columns; and here the organic *versus* inorganic nature of these components will be crucial to the issue of feelings in a way it was not to the issue of conscious thinking. The same consideration will also undermine, I believe, Scriven's argument.

What I mean is this. In 'Reaction B' described above, Simon's friends are imagined dissecting Sally alongside a human cadaver and showing him how different are the materials of which they are constructed. But given their original purpose of fooling Simon, this is too easy. There was no reason for them to give Sally a stomach or sexual glands, for instance; so that if Simon knows anything of human anatomy it would be insane for him to suppose after the dissection that Sally really had pangs of hunger or lustful urges in her former 'life'. It would not be logically contradictory, of course, but it would still be insane. Suppose, however, that for some unspecified reason Simon's friends had gone much farther in their work before he discovered the truth. Suppose they had constructed a mannequin complete with the mechanical equivalent of a functioning stomach, sexual glands, and so on. In this version Sally – let us call her 'R. Sally III' – really can digest food, secrete certain fluids, etc. Here the task of convincing Simon that she had no feelings must be far more difficult. Yet – and this is the point roboticists of the extremist school overlook – the logic of the situation has not changed. We are still dealing with a *machine*: otherwise there would be no point in Simon's plea to 'put her back together again'. He is still asking the impossible, i.e. that life be 'restored' to that which never had life; or, more simply, that from a complex mechanical structure there should come feelings, even though not a single component of that structure is or has been correlated with the occurrence of feeling-states. What Simon's friends know, and would try to make clear to him, is that such feeling-states arise in the context of a larger story, a story which has a place for Simon, but none for Sally. It is the story of organic evolution, of the gradual acquisition of organs and sensory equipment requisite to survival in a competitive biological environment. None of Sally's components belong there: they are all outside that story, and no organisation of them can suddenly make them part of it.

So stated, this may still seem too general and perhaps dogmatic. Later on in this book I shall be considering biological evolution in more detail, as it bears on another topic, but for my present purpose it will suffice to single out one kind of feeling-state which illustrates my meaning well enough. We are all aware, for example, that sensations of *pain* have survival importance to many kinds of organisms. They serve to draw attention to injury or disease, to deter us from actions which experience shows lead to these, and to immobilise a damaged or infected part of the body. I am not saying pain is universally useful, of course: often it is most intense when disease or injury is already fatal. But without it the growing organism is, especially when lacking much instinctive apparatus, almost defenceless against its environment. This is particularly true of highly mobile 'soft' organisms moving about in a world of hard objects: precisely the situation of land-mammals such as men. Indeed it seems impossible to understand the evolution of many biological entities, such as human beings, without the frequent occurrence of painful sensations to them.*

* Professor Antony Flew has pointed out to me in correspondence that it is possible for organisms to evolve into complex forms without pain sensations provided they have very strong withdrawal dispositions linked to most of the stimuli which in fact cause pain. There is certainly no logical obstacle to imagining this. However it seems to me there are scientific difficulties. Animals

Pain, in brief, is just what we have every reason to expect in 'a mass of cells and things' organised into an 'information-system'. But is it also what we could reasonably expect in 'a mass of wires and valves' contrived to simulate a parahuman information-system?

True, some parts of the present human body can be replaced by mechanisms without affecting our belief that the subject has feelings. And MacKay makes much of this fact. He suggests it might be possible even to replace the human brain, gradually, with an identically organised 'artificial brain'. But of course the brain is not itself sensitive; such a man would not be an artificial person, but a natural person with an artificial brain. In theory a heart, a stomach, and many other organs could be replaced by substitute mechanisms. But to get a situation analogous to the one we are considering *the whole nervous system* must be replaced in this way, and every cell, body fluid, and so forth as well. My question is how one could credit the relevant entity with feelings if *none* of its constituent elements ever developed as part of an organic system in which some feeling-states – such as pain – have a natural and scientifically understandable place. Valves, wires, electrodes, transistors: these are all composed of elements from the 'hard' objects among which 'soft' organisms had to navigate without fatal damage to themselves in the long history of evolution. No organisation of the former, no matter how ingenious from a technical point of view, can lead on to a reasonable ascription of feeling-states to them. Sensations of pain arise from contact *with* them in the course of evolution; to suppose that once they are properly organised pain will also occur *to* them is just to close one's eyes to their nature. It is in this connection,

---

with such powerful 'withdrawal dispositions' are precisely those lacking highly differentiated nervous systems, i.e. those which, given a superb instinctive apparatus, do not take up the mobile predatory way of life and do not evolve into intelligent organisms. (See Chapter 4 below.)

rather than in relation to conscious 'thinking', that the disparity between ourselves and machines becomes important.

The choice of pain-sensations as a paradigm case leads back to the larger issue of person-status for machines. MacKay, for example, suggests it might be enough for us to play chess with a machine in order to count it a person. Just as we do not play against a human's body, or even his brain, but against 'him'; so an agreement to play against a chess-playing automaton presupposes a commitment to regard that entity in personal terms. And this is not, according to MacKay, to skip a step. We do not have *first* to discover 'whether a chess-playing mechanism has a personality, or is nothing but a mass of wires and valves'.[6] This seems to me completely false. The question is not: 'Does this chess-playing mechanism have a personality?' (In a weak sense even roulette wheels, I am told, have that.) The question is rather: 'Does this chess-playing mechanism have feelings, so that I can count it a person?' And here the really crucial test would be whether it can suffer, not merely injury, but pain.* Suppose I play with a machine and lose, then smash the machine in anger. Would this have the same moral and legal implications as, say, shooting a human opponent? If my analysis above is sound, there would be no doubt about how to answer. For even if we suppose consciousness in the machine's ratiocinative operations, there is no moral issue here. Let us grant for a moment that when the machine is deciding between, say, R × Kt and R–Q3 it actually says to itself 'Now if I take the Knight he'll probably reply . . .' Seeing the danger ahead I cleverly kick in its conditional switching apparatus and pull out its record storage for good measure. This would be awfully unsporting, but how can one say it is *immoral* with reference to the

* Jeremy Bentham put the same point very aptly in a note to his discussion of cruelty towards animals – see note to §1,4 of chapter 17 of the *Principles of Morals and Legislation* (Blackwell ed.) p. 412 – where he says: 'The question is not "can they *reason*?" nor, "can they *talk*?" but, "can they *suffer*?" ' (I owe this quotation to Professor Flew.)

machine? To claim that you have to suppose these destructive acts actually cause pain to the machine and an end to further feelings.

This point can be illustrated more dramatically by reviving our lady robot. To give the illustration its full force, let us incorporate two possibilities already suggested. First, we shall have Sally in her third form, as containing mechanical equivalents of all the human organs and nervous system. Second, we shall give R. Sally III the benefit of any doubts and suppose she ratiocinates consciously and has learned the language of feelings. Now Simon comes home one day and finds her, not inert on the bathroom floor, but *in flagrante delicto* with his best friend (presumably a computer technician). After chasing his friend out of the house he sets about beating Sally and finally plunges the kitchen knife into her breast several times. He then telephones the police and confesses. Should Simon be indicted for murder? He certainly destroyed Sally, but on the other hand she was never 'living' to begin with: so he cannot have killed her. (The question whether he should be arraigned for 'intent to kill' is exceedingly puzzling.) But he did bring to an end her presumed conscious thoughts: is this not grave enough?

What we have to understand in this imaginary situation is that Sally does not have what I called before a 'unitary mental life'. She can *think*: 'Simon is now going to do this' or 'He refuses to do that'. She can *say*: 'Don't do that, Simon, you're hurting me!' or 'Let's do that again, Simon, it was fun!' But the words 'hurting' and 'fun' cannot have the same meaning to her as to Simon. She can *use* them, as alternative ways of expressing changes in her internal states: this is what tricks Simon into believing she has similar feelings. But because none of her constituent elements, no matter how ingeniously simulative of human antomy, is such that feeling-states could arise from them, she has learned this language of feelings in quite another way than Simon. Admittedly it is difficult to conceive a robot like Sally, which attaches the same consciousness to its ratiocinative functions as you and I do, but always uses feeling-language without any conscious experience of the feelings it refers to. Nevertheless the destruction of such an entity amounts to no more than arresting its conscious ratiocinative processes. I see no direct moral implication in this whatsoever. What makes a human being's death tragic, or at least often sad, is not so much the cessation of thought as the loss of all feeling, all emotion, all sensation. It is this we mourn, and cannot reasonably expect to result from the destruction of a machine.

On the issue of feelings, then, we seem to have reached a logical limit to machine technology. A machine can think (and possibly think consciously), be intelligent, arrive at original solutions to problems, modify its responses in accord with experience, assimilate human language – including the language of sensations and emotions – and even be self-reproducing.* But so long as it is truly a *machine* it will not have feelings.

A final answer to the position of Scriven and MacKay can now be formulated along the following lines. First, we saw at the end of the previous chapter that there can be extra-human persons because 'X is a moral agent, but not a human being' is not self-contradictory: it having been argued that persons are always moral agents and vice versa. The test of whether a machine could be a person is therefore whether it could under any circumstances be counted a moral agent. Second, it was found in the course of that chapter that a moral agent is characteristically both moral subject and moral object. Now the peculiarity of a parahuman robot like Sally is that she can 'take a moral attitude' like other moral subjects. She can say 'Don't do this' or 'Do that', so that she may be said to be making prescriptive statements which are also universalisable. But if she cannot have feelings she cannot be a moral object. She cannot be a moral object because without a

---

* John von Neumann demonstrated the theoretical possibility of mechanical self-replication in his 1951 essay, 'The General and Logical Theory of Automata', in *Cerebral Mechanisms in Behavior*, ed. T. A. Jefferies (New York, 1951) pp. 1-31. There is no question in this of *feelings* associated with organic reproduction.

capacity for pain or pleasure, joy or sorrow, nothing that happens to her will have moral implications. There are, as we saw, many moral objects which are not moral subjects, but there are no moral agents not themselves moral objects. Thus even the most idealised humanoid machine, if it is really a machine, cannot qualify as a person. What really cuts a machine off from the community of persons is not, therefore, a necessary lack of consciousness, but a highly probable lack of feeling.

At the beginning of this chapter I said we would be examining *two* kinds of entities which, if they met all the conceptual requirements for person-status and existed, would be artificial persons. In contrast with machines, the second of these candidates does, as I hope to show in what follows, meet those conceptual requirements. But whether any members of its class actually exist or could come to exist in the foreseeable future is problematic. My excuse for devoting a few pages at the end of this chapter to so hypothetical a possibility is merely that I feel I should give some content now to the concept of an extra-human person.

The very idea of an organic artifact will seem far-fetched to many of my readers. We understand well enough what it is like to graft living organs to existing natural organisms: that is already being done in a modest way for medical and experimental purposes. It takes only a fair share of technological optimism to envisage constructing a superior organism by such means. But this would be a patchwork organism, not a true artifact. Similarly, one can imagine large-scale substitution of more powerful and efficient mechanisms for present human organs: but the result is less of an organism though more of an artifact. A true 'organic artifact' must therefore be entirely organic in its components and entirely artificial in its construction. Given this extreme if noncontroversial characterisation of the entity, one can do very little to indicate how it would come into being. I shall limit myself to two suitably vague suggestions. First, it would be necessary to create organic materials in a laboratory from non-organic materials. The initial steps in that direction have already been taken (more on this in the next chapter, in a less hypothetical context), though of course one is a very long way from what is needed for our illustration. Second, and assuming that cellular tissue of artificial origins is now available, one must suppose that complete control of the 'genetic code' has been attained, so that within certain limits the organism will grow as one wants it to. Assuming these two conditions satisfied, we can loosely conceive the theoretical possibility of developing true organic artifacts according to specifications.

What specifications are desirable? That will depend on the designers' intentions, of course, yet some possibilities can be fairly easily excluded. It would not be practicable to produce a biologically inferior race of slaves, for example, since any society technologically capable of this would have long since developed far cheaper and more efficient computer-based machines to do all heavy labour, menial tasks, and so on. Nor would it be desirable to produce a biologically superior race. Any species capable of doing so could be relied on to use this knowledge for improvement of itself, rather than creating its own potential conquerors. So that if one rules out these two extremes it seems likely organic artifacts produced in large numbers, and not merely for experimental purposes, would be produced on biological parity to the parent species if at all. I shall leave entirely aside the question *why* any species would want to do this.

So much for the background of our problem. Now I want to ask what the conceptual implications of this hypothetical exercise are. We have an entity, let us say in this case parahuman or humanoid, which has a genetic structure nearly identical to that of *Homo sapiens*, but is not human because it is an artifact. In fact we can go further and suppose that for some reason its creators are not satisfied until they achieve a truly isomorphic species, ruthlessly destroying all embryos which fail to duplicate its own genetic code. In this case our humanoids soon become indistinguishable from the parent species in the embryonic stage and are henceforth able to develop and reproduce just as humans do. Once we have a few families of these entities functioning, they can be adopted by the human community, their children sent to our schools, and so on. In time they become thoroughly assimilated to human society. Some become well-known athletes, doctors, entertainers, biologists even. Others write novels or paint, adopt political causes. In short, there ceases to be any criterion for distinguishing between ourselves and them other than knowledge of their ancestors' origins, which reduces to some dusty files in a laboratory somewhere. All objective standards for discrimination have disappeared. Unless we want to brand them on the foreheads or in some other way provide unmistakable distinguishing criteria, one would never know if one is talking to a descendant of the original class of isomorphic humanoid artifacts or not. Let us call this Case I.

In Case II we do not aim for genetic isomorphism, but for a species on biological parity with *Homo sapiens*, yet distinct from it. To preserve this distinction biologically the genetic code relating to sexual reproduction is altered so that if members of the new species mate with humans no offspring will result. In this way we are sure there will not occur, as in Case I, an eventual assimilation to the human species. And in order to make casual distinctions easy, we arrange the genetic structure so that all members of the new species will have, say, eight toes on each foot, green pigmentation of the skin, and purple hair. But in all other respects the species resembles our own and has the same biological advantages we have. Its members have, for example, a large cranial capacity, slowly developing and highly convoluted brain, long period of gestation and of parent dependency: all factors, in other words, favourable to the development of 'objective language', or the manipulation of symbols and assimilation of a conceptual scheme. The descendants of this species are then treated exactly as in Case I, except that, as we saw, they cannot be absorbed into our species and we are never in doubt about their origins. The result is that they achieve the same levels of education, professional service, artistic and scientific originality as in the other case. They might even embrace the same political causes, though having, of course, a special concern for the welfare of their own community. *Social* assimilation to humanity is thus presumed, or at least envisaged, in this picture. The contrast between this situation and the preceding one might be summed up as follows: in the former we had biological integration; in the latter we have biological separation, but equality.

But in either version there is a factor unmentioned so far which needs to be stressed now. I mean that only the *first*-generation members of these species were really 'organic artifacts'. All of their descendants from that point on were natural organisms as much as any human being is. Indeed one can say that in Case I all succeeding members actually became, or at least were already potentially, members of the human race. To call any of them 'parahuman' or 'humanoid' after that is biologically misleading. In Case II the descendants cease to be artifacts, again, though they remain biologically distinct from humans thereafter. In so far as they are very much like humans in other respects, one may continue to call them 'humanoid' or 'parahuman' (but in time they might resent this proprietary term and insist on another designation). Thus it is the first generation in both cases which is 'extra-human', because its members are artifacts rather than natural organisms; after that only the descendants described in Case II are extra-human, and no longer artifacts at all. Taking just these, there remains only the question whether they would also be 'persons'.

On the criteria set out in this book, there seems no way to deny them this status. For as I have described organic artifacts and their descendants here, they can not only do everything humans do, but also be credited with feelings. If we go back to the MacKay chart and substitute first-generation organic artifacts for machines in the right-hand inner column under 'ARTIFICIAL', we have no difference between what appears there and what appears in the left-hand inner column except at the very top, which will read 'constructed' as opposed to 'grown'. And if anyone balks at according feelings to something constructed, we need only refer to the progeny of the Case II artifacts, who are 'grown' just as you and I are. We have no better reason for denying sensations and emotional states to these entities than we should have for denying them to another human being. Therefore *all* of the typical P-predicates have a reasonable and non-misleading application to them. They *would* be moral objects because they could feel pain, suffer unhappiness, and so on; and for the same reason they would be moral agents, capable of moral relationships with other moral agents. What are they then but extra-human persons?

One can always invoke private and special criteria, of course. One can say only people with souls are true persons, and that God would never bestow souls on organic artifacts and their descendants, especially since they owe their creation to God's own sinful creatures. But I doubt that even this claim will withstand analysis. It is true that the entities we are considering were designed rather than evolved over a long period of time, but I see no grounds for supposing God a champion of evolution. If humans are themselves descended from 'lower' and presumably soulless animals, then God could just as well choose to insert souls in these 'artificial' creatures at some future time as He did to insert souls in humans when they appeared. Their being creatures of sinful man poses no special problems either. As I have described them they are morally no better and no worse than their human designers. Surely some of them could become Christians too? Or Moslems? Or Jews? If they have not only biological but moral parity with human beings, it seems the lowest form of theological discrimination to deny them the very possibility of eternal salvation.

A concluding note will now serve to lead into the next chapters of this book. While in the last section of this chapter I have tried to give theoretical flesh to the concept of an extra-human person, I was careful to say it is highly unlikely we shall encounter organic artifacts like these in the foreseeable future. No serious existential question about them therefore arises. However I was also careful to avoid ruling out entirely the actuality of their existence. As the sub-title of my book indicates, it is my larger purpose to survey the possible existence of moral agents in the universe: anywhere and of any sort. And it is conceivable, as the coming chapters will argue, that more developed societies of persons exist in the universe which could, therefore, have already created such artificial entities. So they may, after all, exist. But if such entities exist, it will only be through discovery of the existence of their creators that we shall have, for a very long time at least, any knowledge of them at all. Thus the possible existence of organic artifacts or their descendants is wholly subordinate to the question whether, in the first instance, there exist *naturally evolved* extra-human persons elsewhere in the universe.

This is the question I shall be taking up now.

1. In *Minds and Machines*, reprinted in *Dimensions of Mind*, ed. S.Hook (Collier-Macmillan, 1961) pp. 153-4 especially.

2. See R.Puccetti, 'Can Humans Think?', in *Analysis*, XXVI, no. 6 (June 1966).

3. 'The Compleat Robot: A [*sic*] Prolegomena to Androidology', reprinted in *Dimensions of Mind*, ed. S.Hook, pp. 113-33. See also Scriven's *Computers and Comprehension*, co-authored with M.Kochen, D.MacKay, M.E.Maron, and L.Uhr (Rand Corporation, 1964), especially pp. 2-7. Quotations are from both these publications.

4. 'The Use of Behavioural Language to Refer to Mechanical Processes', in *British Journal for the Philosophy of Science*, L (1962) 89–103.

5. Namely by Scriven's collaborators in *Computers and Comprehension*, p. 7.

6. MacKay, in *British Journal for the Philosophy of Science*, L (1962) 98.

E

3 *Extraterrestrial Persons: I*

THE previous chapter closed with the question whether there are naturally evolved extra-human persons in the universe. But as this is perhaps too sweeping a question to be answered within the confines of a single chapter, I shall break it into two parts. I shall ask first what grounds, if any, there are to suppose that intelligent organisms have evolved elsewhere than on the Earth; and second, assuming a favourable treatment of the first question, what claim such beings would have to person-status and what kind of relations we could possibly have with them. The former will be taken up here, the latter in the next chapter. A certain amount of overlapping between the two is unavoidable, as we shall see, but I will do my best to keep them separate.

Belief in the existence of extraterrestrial forms of life, including intelligent beings, has a long, if spotty, history. Hints of this belief may be found, for example, in certain canonical documents of the Jain religion dating back to 300 B.C. (a point I shall return to in the last chapter of this book). The ancient Atomists and their successors the Epicureans, of course, believed in the plurality of worlds inhabited by intelligent organisms. Teng Mu, a scholar of the Sung Dynasty, is reported to have expressed such a belief. During the Renaissance in Europe, as we all know, Giordano Bruno went up in smoke for teaching the same: though with a mystical and theological twist. Among contemporaries the Rosicrucian cult advocates this idea, but again in a mystical context and coupled with other doctrines, such as the existence of a Cosmic Mind.

What distinguishes all these speculative surmises is precisely their unscientific character. Even the ancient Atomists, despite their mechanistic bent and crude yet startling anticipations of many modern scientific discoveries, really had no 'good reasons' – by contemporary standards of evidence – for teaching the multiplicity of worlds and intelligent beings. This is obvious from the fact that it would have been equally consistent with their fundamental atomism, and not at all inconsistent with any observations they could make, to suppose the visible planets and stars small conglomerations of atoms circling an unmoving Earth at a short distance away: with similar small conglomerations extending beyond sight throughout an infinite area of surrounding space. That the Atomists chose a contrary interpretation of the available data says much for their imaginative powers, but nothing for their scientific acumen.

The emergence of a scientific basis for belief in extraterrestrial life and intelligence is in fact only very recent. Historically speaking, I suppose one can regard this as a continuation, and perhaps a final fulfilment, of the Copernican Revolution. One can say Copernicus' theory led to a spatial decentralisation of the Earth, as Darwin's evolutionary hypothesis led to a temporal decentralisation of Man's biological history. Taken together, these twin blows against anthropocentrism opened the way to seeing advanced forms of life on Earth as but incidental occurrences in a cosmic evolutionary process. But in fact this neat generalisation is misleading. For between the publication of Darwin's *Origin of Species* and the present day there occurred two scientific developments which seemed fatal to any pat assumption of universal organic evolution and which, therefore, retarded fulfilment of the Copernican Revolution by almost a hundred years.

The first phase in this reactionary process occurred in biology, where Pasteur's work showed that even microbes could not be generated spontaneously from inanimate matter, but only from other living microbes. That was in 1863, and from then until a few decades ago it was sufficient to discourage attempts to extend Darwinian concepts backwards in time and to bridge the gap – at least theoretically – between the living and the non-living.

All this began to change, however, with the appearance of Oparin's book *The Origin of Life* in 1936. By the mid-1950s the experimental work of Miller, Urey, and others, following the theoretical lead of Oparin, had given us a picture in terms of which we can now conceive in a general way, at least, the spontaneous generation of living molecules from inanimate matter.[1] What we have to do is postulate a primitive terrestrial atmosphere consisting of hydrogen, carbon combined with hydrogen as methane, oxygen combined with hydrogen as water, and nitrogen combined with hydrogen in the form of ammonia. Now we need some force or forces to separate the atoms in these primitive molecules, so thay may re-combine to form more complex molecules. There are three obvious candidates for this role: lightning, the sun's ultraviolet light, and ionising radiation from either cosmic sources or radioactive elements on the Earth's primitive surface. The experiments mentioned above were designed to simulate these conditions, and succeeded in converting those simple molecules into formic acid, acetic acid, succinic acid, and glycine: the very molecules of which living things are constructed today. Amino acids, sugars, fats: these are just the bottom of the organic ladder. There is a long way to go to cell formation* and the sort of chemical structure which permits Darwinian principles to take over, and not all the intervening rungs in the ladder are understood. But at least what seemed an unbridgeable gap between the living and the non-living has had a few strong strands thrown across it.

The question then arises: 'If life generated spontaneously on the Earth's surface some two to three thousand million years ago, why not elsewhere?' The first place one would think of looking, of course, would be on the surface of our familiar planetary

* However see footnote on page 83.

companions, since they are equally old and subject to the same kind of solar radiation. And before very long we shall certainly be able to examine some of them quite closely. In fact we have something to go on even now, for extraterrestrial material comes to us all the time in the form of meteoric infall. Some recent analyses of meteorite fragments do seem to reveal hydrocarbon-like materials and other features associated with nucleic acid and the amino acids,[2] though the evidence is not entirely conclusive. But of course the existence of extraterrestrial life *per se* has limited interest when confined to our own solar system, for there is no question of highly evolved, intelligent organisms on the other planets. Temperatures on Venus, for example, are so high that only anaerobic microtype organisms could exist there, suspended in its surrounding cloud-layers. On Mars the scarcity of oxygen and formidable temperature variations limit evolution to the simplest and hardiest forms of life. All the other planetary bodies and their satellites are even more surely excluded: surface temperatures being either far too hot or far too cold. (This may not be true of Jupiter or Saturn, but they have no oxygen.) The development of intelligent life, then, comparable to what appeared on Earth's surface, can be expected, if at all, only on bodies outside our solar system. Which is to say that extraterrestrial life of the most interesting kind must also be extrasolar.

This observation brings us to the second 'reactionary' phase of post-Darwinian science, which occurred in astrophysical theory during the first third of our present century. For during that period there was a resurgence of the 'dualistic' theory accounting for formation of our planetary system. As put forward by Chamberlin and Moulton and later elaborated by Jeffrys and Jeans, this theory held that in the distant past another star careened close to our sun, raising by its gravitational attraction a tidal bulge and drawing out from it a filament of gas which then broke up into gas spheres; upon condensation these became our sun's planetary bodies. Now given the enormous distance between the stars in proportion to their magnitudes, it was easy to see that formation of a planetary system must be an extremely rare event: a happy chance on a par with, say, hitting an eagle with a pea-shooter. Given this rarity, the possibility of there being other planetary systems on which life could arise seemed so remote that it is no wonder scientists continued to regard belief in extraterrestrial intelligence as purely speculative.

However, this situation began to change about three decades ago, when the dualistic theory met a series of setbacks. Among the difficulties noted were these: that our sun's planetary orbits are far too extensive for the 'cooled filament' thesis, 98 per cent of the solar system's angular momentum being concentrated in the planets' orbital motion; that the high temperature of the filament upon ejection would cause it to disperse in space rather than condense; and that in any case such a filament would be dispersed by shearing in the tidal field of the sun.[3] As a result of these criticisms there was a widespread return to the earlier 'monistic' theory of Descartes, Kant, and Laplace, given new elaboration by von Weizsäcker, Urey, and others. In terms of this view our sun and its planets formed simultaneously out of a giant 'parent nebula' of gas and dust four and one-half thousand million years ago, and for this to happen no odd chance of a passing star need be supposed.

But of course this changes the whole picture of planetary occurrence in the universe. Leaving aside binary and multiple star-systems, which would make stable planetary orbits difficult, a full 20 per cent of all visible stars are single like our Sun. And of these one quarter are large enough, but not too large, to provide enduring 'habitable' temperature zones for their planets. So that if life generates spontaneously from non-living materials under conditions similar to those prevailing on our Earth's surface two to three thousand million years ago, and such stars are of at least equal age as the Sun (in fact the galaxy as a whole is from ten to fifteen thousand million years old), then we have every reason to expect our cosmos to have a universal biochemistry just as it has a universal physics and chemistry. Which means that life, and possibly intelligent life, is really a fairly common development in the universe rather than an extremely accidental and therefore almost unique one.

Such is the scientific basis, at any rate, for the new optimism concerning extraterrestrial intelligence. But formidable problems remain if this attitude is to take on more than a merely hypothetical plausibility. To return to my opening image of this development as a continuation of, and perhaps a fulfilment of, the Copernican Revolution, one striking difference between it and the two preceding 'states' must be noted. The Copernican hypothesis was eminently testable, even if the theory's final confirmation was not technically possible until optical telescopes sufficiently powerful to detect a stellar parallax were developed in the early nineteenth century. Similarly, Darwinian evolutionary theory was always testable in principle, though almost three-quarters of a century elapsed before the mechanism of mutation was isolated and demonstrated under laboratory conditions. The hypothesis that extraterrestrial (really extrasolar) intelligent life exists is quite another matter. Confirmation of this hypothesis depends, as we shall see, upon special considerations left entirely open by the scientific evidence in its favour. What is more, there is one important respect in which the hypothesis cannot be 'tested' at all, even on the most optimistic assumptions. These peculiarities raise a more general problem, which might be designated the question of 'the logical status of belief in extraterrestrial intelligence', and which I shall be discussing at some length in what follows.

The best way to approach this problem is to set out a series of claims concerning the existence of extraterrestrial intelligence, starting with what I shall call 'extremely soft' claims and ranging downwards to 'hard' claims. This distinction is largely one of degree, but at certain points the difference greatly affects the issue of confirmability, hence the logical status of the claim itself.

Case I. Suppose someone says, just as a point of argument, that it is ridiculous to imagine our sun the only star in this vast universe with an inhabited planet. (Many of the pre-scientific and contemporary unscientific claims one encounters take this form.) Here we are on the periphery of one galaxy among thousands of millions, each containing from one to two hundred thousand million stars. Surely a few of these stars, or at least one, in that vast panorama has a planet capable of supporting life; and on its surface there may have evolved intelligent beings. To regard our sun as an absolutely unique stellar phenomenon is certainly a case of cosmic provincialism.

This argument has a persuasive ring to it, but unfortunately the very vastness of the universe, from which it derives its plausibility, renders confirmation of the claim practically hopeless. For if there were only a *few* stars like this it becomes statistically probable that none of them would be in our galaxy or indeed anywhere in our galactic neighbourhood. We must remember that there are at least 10^{10} galaxies: assuming an even distribution of stars having planets, any small number would be scattered among them on a ratio of something like one for each one hundred galaxies. Which means that the nearest habitable planet would be so far away we could observe its parent star, if at all, only as it was several thousand million years ago: at a time when the Earth was hardly formed. With regard to stars like our own sun, this means they could not yet have life on their planets; and worse, if they did have inhabited planets, we could never be sure they still do, after so long a time.

Case II. A slightly less 'soft' claim arises, ironically, from a scientific partisan's attempt to show how unreasonable it is to deny the probable existence of extraterrestrial (again, really extrasolar) life-bearing planets. I must stipulate that this calculation does not reflect his view of the probable occurrence of such planets – as we shall see later on he gives higher possible values for extraterrestrial life than any recent serious writer on the subject – but only an exercise in statistical conservatism designed to break down resistance to the whole idea.

The scientist I have in mind is Harlow Shapley. Shapley asks us to suppose there are only 10^{20} stars in the visible universe (10^{21} is the minimal figure estimated by most astronomers today). Of these 10^{20} stars let us say only one in a hundred is a single star, allowing stable planetary orbits. But of all single stars let us suppose only one in a hundred actually has a planetary system. Of these only one in a hundred has a planet really like the Earth; of these only one in a hundred is situated in that interval called the 'liquid-water belt' (neither too hot nor too cold); and of these only one in a hundred has a really suitable surface chemistry. That still leaves ten thousand million habitable planets in the universe.[4]

Now if someone was to base his claim for the existence of extraterrestrial intelligence (which Shapley does not) on this formula, we would not be much better off than in the previous case. For the final number of claimed sites is only 10^{10}, which is the estimated number of observable galaxies. This gives us one stellar candidate per galaxy. And since we have already used our chance in the Milky Way, that means the nearest inhabited planet would still be not only extrasolar but extragalactic. As it happens our very closest (spiral) galactic neighbour is the M31 nebula in Andromeda, two million light years away. So that anything we might possibly observe taking place there would be two million years old. It is possible, of course, that intelligent life did appear that long ago elsewhere, but if we take our own species' history as the norm (and it seems we must in the absence of comparative data), then two difficulties arise. First, it would be necessary not only that intelligent life should have appeared, but also that it should have evolved to the level of a very advanced technological civilisation, capable of making its presence known across intergalactic space, in two million years' less time than it took for mankind to appear. Second, our own experience of civilisation is only a few thousand years long, and of technological civilisation but a few decades: yet we have already seen how fraught with danger it can be. Detection of the existence of such a society two million years ago in another galaxy could hardly provide, then, any assurance of its continued existence today. In general it is probably safe to say that any claim about the *contemporary* existence of extraterrestrial intelligence which implies extragalactic *loci* is unconfirmable in the strict sense, given the distances it involves, not only in practice, but also in principle.

Case III. Surprisingly, a still harder claim is permitted by the very same 'dualistic' theory of planetary formation which did so much to retard scientific interest in the possibility of extraterrestrial intelligence. For even on the now-discredited Jeans hypothesis one star in fifty million might in its lifetime collide with or closely approach another, giving rise in the latter instance to a tidal bulge. Taking into account other factors, it is possible on this view that our own galaxy would contain as many as ten or more planetary systems. This reduces the distance between our Earth and other possible sites of intelligent life to several thousand light years. With a reduction on that scale, our situation has definitely improved, for it is quite plausible that intelligent life should be a mere few thousand – or even tens of thousands – of years ahead of us elsewhere. We have no right to suppose our record is the *minimum* time necessary for evolution of intelligence and technology, but only the norm. And of course it is not entirely unwarranted to presume that a civilisation capable of making its presence known to us within our galaxy continues to survive throughout the time it takes for us to receive information of it. Thus confirmation of a claim based on such considerations is certainly possible in principle.

One must wonder why, if this is so, the 'dualistic' theory led to such pessimistic conclusions about extraterrestrial life and intelligence. The answer is that confirmability 'in principle' is not enough, obviously, to excite scientific interest in an hypothesis. All kinds of assertions are confirmable in principle: such as the existence of sea-monsters and centaurs. But when an assertion is so lacking in specific content, so devoid of observational directions, that confirmability in practice is not really a definite prospect for scientific inquiry, then there is just no point in getting excited about it. And, in fact, this is the case with the claim we are considering. To say there are even twenty possible sites for extraterrestrial intelligence in our galaxy is not to provide us with any particular empirical expectations. The statement is circumscribed only by the galaxy as a whole, which contains $(1-2) \times 10^{11}$ stars. Assuming again an even distribution of these limited possible sites, that would mean the nearest is situated around one of the two or three million stars in our immediate galactic vicinity. But which one? It would take about seven years just to *look* at that many stars for one second each. And of course one could not 'see' anything that would confirm this hypothesis anyway, no matter how powerful one's telescopes are. We can be fairly certain that if belief in extraterrestrial intelligence were confirmed in spite of this sparse distribution of likely sites, it would be a most incredibly lucky chance and not at all the result of any specific efforts we made to confirm it. Rather it would be the result of such beings taking extraordinary steps to probe the sun as a possible site, beings possessed of a technology far in advance of anything we can now envisage.

Case IV. The claim I am about to consider is not only 'hard': it is the one which underlies current scientific interest in extraterrestrial intelligence. You will recall that I alluded earlier to the conviction growing among scientists that about 5 per cent of all visible stars are both single – hence capable of providing stable planetary orbits – and of the right size to creat 'habitable' temperature zones for the spontaneous generation and evolution of life.

One of the principal proponents of this view is Su-Shu Huang.[5] He has pointed out that the larger and more luminous a star, the greater the probability that one of its planets (if any) would orbit in the habitable zone. Among the 'main-sequence' stars, comprising about 90 per cent of all single stars, the smaller ones (late K and M stars on the scale) provide only a very narrow band of habitable temperatures; while the large early spectral types (O, B, A, and early F), with broad habitable zones, unfortunately evolve too quickly themselves for biological evolution to take place on whatever planets they might have. This reduces stellar candidates for extraterrestrial intelligence to the moderately small stars (late F, G, and early K) of which our own Earth is typical. Now by a striking coincidence, Huang argues, the rapid axial rotation of main-sequence stars stops abruptly near spectral type F5 on the descending scale. This strongly suggests the transfer of angular momentum to a planetary system for all single stars below that size. Not all astrophysicists agree with this inference,[6] but most do. Thus it becomes plausible that nearly all main-sequence single stars below size F5 and perhaps above K5 have not only planetary systems, but broad habitable temperature zones sustained quite long enough to have evolved higher forms of intelligent life.

If this is a sound surmise, the prospects for confirming belief in the existence of extraterrestrial intelligence are greatly increased. For this would mean our galaxy contains one hundred million (some writers give ten times this estimate) stellar candidates at least, located at a distance of some 50 to 80 light years from each other. Thus the time factors mentioned before would have no practical significance, either with regard to the evolution of intelligent life or its persistence through the period that information is being transmitted to us. Nor should we have to scan all the stars in our corner of the galaxy in looking for possible sites of intelligent life: instead we could concentrate on single stars of the late F, G, and early K spectral range. As Huang showed, most of the stars within our immediate solar neighbourhood are M-dwarfs and late K types, binaries and multiples. If we eliminate these and white dwarfs, as well as high-velocity visitors, that leaves only two – Epsilon Eridani and Tau Ceti – of the forty-one stars nearest our sun to a distance of five parsecs (about 16 light years) which fit the description given. Of course one wants a larger member of stellar candidates for extraterrestrial intelligence than just two; in order to increase our chances of confirming the hypothesis we shall need to consider stars at distances of 100 to 500 light years. But even so we should know, on this view, which ones to study: and that is an enormous advance over our previous situation.

I have not yet discussed what, exactly, one looks for in attempting to confirm this hypothesis. Before I do that, however, let us consider a final case, the 'hardest' claim yet made.

Case V. I said earlier that Harlow Shapley gives higher possible values for the occurrence of extraterrestrial life than any writer on this subject. That is due to his suggestion, made a few years ago, that invisible heavenly bodies must be far more numerous than visible ones.[7] A star seventy times larger than the sun would probably explode, but below that limit there is a continuous gradation. However, large stars are scarce, medium and moderately small ones (like our Sun) are more common, and small stars are abundant. In other words, the farther one goes down the scale of sizes the more numerous they become: which suggests there are vast numbers of stars too small to give off solar radiation, hence invisible optically. Similarly, there may be very distant large planets of similar size in the same situation, except that they are orbitally dependent upon some large star. In either case, Shapley reasons, such intermediate-sized bodies would be quite warm from internal radioactive decay. Some of these, then, would be of the critical size – say ten times the mass of our planet Jupiter – where their surfaces would be crusted and water could be retained in liquid form. Even without sunlight, this internally produced energy should be sufficient for chemical evolution and photosynthesis of a distinct sort. Thus life could be generated on such crusted stars and self-heating distant planets; and if so, why should not intelligent beings evolve there?

Now if this suggestion is accepted it would certainly improve our expectation of encountering extraterrestrial intelligence some day. For recent calculations[8] show there are about sixty invisible bodies (down to the size of Mars) for each visible star in the heavens. Thus even though no such body is near enough to our solar system to have an observable effect on the outer planets, there may be a great number between us and the nearest star we can see. Eventually we should be able to locate them, in spite of their invisibility, by using large radio telescopes sensitive to their intense (infrared) radiation.

In what follows, however, I am going to discount Case V altogether. This is because, as Shapley admits, gravitational forces on the surfaces of such small crusted stars or large self-heating planets would be simply enormous. Under such conditions it is extremely unlikely that anything but rudimentary oceanic life could evolve. I am not saying it is impossible that intelligent beings should develop there, but in the absence of really plausible and concrete suggestions along those lines I think we must exclude such bodies from further consideration.

Returning now to the situation described in Case IV, let us ask how in fact one might hope, on that basis, to confirm the hypothetical existence of extraterrestrial intelligent beings. Remember that we have established only two things: (1) that about 5 per cent of all single stars are of the right size to have planetary systems in which one or more planets would fall in the 'habitable' temperature zone for long periods of time; and (2) that life could generate spontaneously and evolve into intelligent forms during that period of time by the same means as obtained on the surface of the Earth. I shall now consider three ways in which one would, perhaps, hope to confirm the hypothesis: by observing these stars, by visiting them, and by receiving signals from them.

The first can be disposed of very quickly. At a distance of ten parsecs (about 32 light years) and in the orbital plane of the planetary system, it would be impossible to detect a planet the size of Jupiter except by accident, even if one presupposes far greater measurement precisions than our present ones.[9] But suppose one could detect planets around another star. What could one expect to see at stellar distances that would constitute evidence of intelligent life? Even at one hundred miles above the Earth one can no longer distinguish cities or bridges with the naked eye: and it would be absurd to imagine that optical telescopes will ever bring us up that close to the planets of another star. Simple observation of likely stellar candidates in our galactic vicinity affords no hope at all, then, of confirming belief in extraterrestrial intelligence.

Mention of the need to observe such stars very closely, i.e. from their own immediate stellar neighbourhoods, leads into discussion of the second possibility. For many scientists look forward to humans either receiving visits from or visiting extrasolar planetary systems, or at least exchanging instrument-probes with them. And certainly this would be a striking way to validate the hypothesis of extraterrestrial intelligence. But in every variation on this theme the same problem arises, i.e. whether in fact it is feasible to send physical objects – be they living organisms or packages of instruments – from one stellar neighbourhood to another.

Now there is a *prima facie* plausibility to this talk of interstellar travel. For one thing, space travel *per se* is nothing new. Our Earth itself is a kind of spaceship; as the sun's companion it travels ten million miles a day in a path around the galaxy. Like Monsieur Jourdain, we find we've been doing it all our lives. But, of course, so have all our stellar neighbours, and at the same distance from us; the problem is not just to travel through space, but to travel through the space separating us from them in addition to our normal space journey. This leads to a second favourable consideration, our confidence in technological advance. Only a century ago one would not have believed that men could ever fly through the atmosphere, and even fifty years ago it would have seemed insane to suppose we could do that at speeds greater than sound. As for energy sources, who would have said a quarter of a century ago that we might be able to construct 100-megaton thermonuclear weapons? It becomes quite easy, then, to sweep aside all present technological difficulties as merely temporary impediments to interstellar travel. Finally, nothing convinces like success, and the successful beginnings of interplanetary space travel have infected everyone with optimism. This is exemplified in the titles we give to our fledgling space travellers: 'astronaut', or sailors among the stars; and 'cosmonaut', navigator of the cosmos.

Unfortunately for this kind of talk, there remain certain facts about interstellar travel requirements which cannot be glossed over. First there is the question of distances to be covered. It has been pointed out that on a scale of 1:180 thousand million we get a model like this. Our Earth is a barely visible grain of sand revolving around a cherrystone – the Sun – three feet away; other grains of sand, some quite larger than ours, are doing the same as far out as 120 feet beyond us, these being the other planets. Now where is the nearest other cherrystone? It is, on this scale, 140 miles from our grain of sand. But of course there may be no intelligent life on the grains of sand, if any, revolving around it. The nearest interesting cherrystone from that point of view might be 600 miles away. The nearest other group of cherrystones – or galaxy – would on this scale be almost a hundred million miles away. The farthest clusters of cherrystones we have seen so far, by the way, are two thousand times as far as that. However, let us suppose we have good reason to suspect the existence of intelligent extraterrestrials on planets of a reasonably near-by star, say 12 light years distant. How should we go there to see? This leads to the second basic fact about interstellar travel: time and energy requirements for covering such distances.

Several years ago Edward Purcell set out the essential difficulties in 'ideal' interstellar travel, relying solely on the elementary laws of mechanics (though in this case relativistic mechanics).[10] He pointed out that rocket enthusiasts often suppose stellar distances can be easily overcome by technical progress in fuel and engine design plus the 'time-dilation' effect provided by special relativity theory. The latter is certainly an asset for long journeys. If we could get a vehicle up to near the speed of light, time would come to a near stop: in fact all the physical, chemical, and biological processes of its passengers would be enormously retarded.* Thus a round-trip journey to a star 250 parsecs away (about 820 light years) might age the crew by only 27 years while 1550 years have passed on the Earth. Much longer voyages yield fantastic results. For example, a trip to another galaxy and back, which could be accomplished in 60 years' time for the crew, would find the Earth five million years older. But for the 'shorter' journeys we are contemplating in our solar neighbourhood, this effect has less importance. The stellar candidate at a mere 12 light years' distance, for instance, allows a round trip of 28 years' Earth time (including accelerations and decelerations at 1g and reaching a top speed of 99 per cent the velocity of light each way), while only 10 years have passed for the crew. This is a great saving, but since even the time-period on Earth is comfortably within a generation, it will not matter much for our purposes. What does matter is the kind of energy sources needed to reach such speeds: as Purcell notes, it is not a problem of kinematics so much as energetics.

For even in relativistic mechanics there is always a certain relation between initial mass and final mass of the rocket which determines the limits of exhaust velocity in any given case. Thus if one overlooks all technical difficulties it is possible to imagine using a propellant based on ideal nuclear fusion which burns hydrogen to helium with 100 per cent efficiency: yet the exhaust

* Oddly, not every biological scientist is willing to accept this straightforward conclusion from relativistic theory. N.J.Berrill, for example, flatly rejects it, saying it has meaning only in the mathematico-physical world and that organisms age according to their local time-systems. Cf. his *Worlds Without End* (Macmillan, N.Y., 1964) p. 217.

velocity attained would be only one-eighth the velocity of light. To attain a speed of 99 per cent the speed of light with this fuel the initial mass has to be a thousand million times the final mass. Or suppose, Purcell asks, we were somehow able to use nature's best fusion reaction as a propellant: the mutual annihilation of matter and anti-matter. He calculates that to make this voyage to a star 12 light years away from us and come back a 10-ton payload requires a 400,000-ton rocket, half matter and half anti-matter. Quite apart from the problem of containing the anti-matter until one is ready to use it (*in what* would it be contained?), the resultant rocket would radiate 10^{18} watts upon ignition, more than the total power the Earth receives from the sun. But this energy is not sunshine: it is gamma rays. The problem would be not merely to shield the payload, Purcell says, but to shield the Earth. Similarly pessimistic conclusions are reached by Sebastian von Hoerner in his calculations.[11]

However, if one were willing to settle for much slower speeds, there is no doubt we could eventually send a rocket or spaceship to a neighbouring star. The question is whether under such conditions we should ever want to. For the problem then would be the reverse: not so much energetics as kinematics. Von Hoerner shows that with present sources of nuclear energy, such as the fission of uranium, and optimistically supposing a mass ratio of 10, we could hope for one-tenth the speed of light. Time-dilation has almost no effect at such low velocities. Taking into account acceleration and decleration at 1g, the full travel time out and back to a star 12 light years away would be over 300 years. To go far out and back, say to a star some 800 light years away, would take 17,000 years. Yet it may be necessary to go that far to find intelligent life. Or suppose we could use the ideal nuclear fusion of hydrogen into helium. With the same factors in mind it would require, if we were able to get a maximum velocity of one-fifth the speed of light, about 160 years for the shorter round trip and 8000 for the longer. But again time-dilation would be unimportant, since it becomes so only at velocities over one-half the speed of light.

Thus we see that at feasible velocities interstellar travel, or sending instrument-probes to other stellar systems, is entirely unsuitable as a means of confirming the hypothesis of extra-terrestrial intelligence. To do so involves not only an enormous technological development and expense. We should also have to allow either for some sort of 'hibernation' of our space voyagers during centuries, perhaps milleniums; or we should have to be prepared to let them spend generations in an enclosed spaceship for the same purpose. I am not saying we might not ever want to, or be able to, do just that. But surely it is ridiculous to suppose we will do this *merely* in order to test the hypothesis being considered. There is no hypothesis the truth or falsity of which would ever be so important as to justify such efforts, such waste, such potential sacrifice. Yet there are serious scientists who talk as if we might do this some day. One recent writer, for example, actually pictures a trip to a near-by star taking 225 years and seven genera-tions to complete *one* way, without the humans responsible for the undertaking or the spaceship occupants having any idea what they will find.[12] He conveniently terminates this imaginative account upon arrival in the chosen stellar vicinity. (As a matter of fact it is Alpha Centauri, which though very near – 4.3 light years – probably has no stable planets in an habitable temperature zone because it is a triple system whose two massive components have an eccentric binary orbit.) My point is just that all talk of using such means to validate belief in the existence of extra-terrestrial intelligent life has no relation to reality and can have none in any foreseeable technological future.

There remains, fortunately, a third and final possible way of confirming the hypothesis under consideration. For the whole subject of 'interstellar communication' neatly divides into two parts: the sending of physical objects across interstellar spaces, whether spaceships or packages of instruments; and the sending merely of electromagnetic signals across the same distances. The difficulties of the former we have already seen. Transfer of physical objects, at least as a means of spatial investigation, is likely always to be limited to the one cubic light year of space containing our solar system. But electromagnetic communication is quite another matter. Here there is no problem of attaining high velocities or reconciling oneself to centuries-long voyages. All electromagnetic communication is conducted at the speed of light, and the cost of radiating enough electrical energy to send messages to a star 12 light years away is a few shillings. Purcell estimates that even by present techniques we could span three million cubic light years of space by electromagnetic signals, a space which contains five hundred sun-like stars.

However, there are serious difficulties in relying solely upon electromagnetic communication to confirm the hypothesis of extraterrestrial intelligence. But before I go into these let me stress that we have no choice. There simply is no other way to validate the hypothesis in any technological future we may reasonably anticipate. For our presumed galactic neighbours are at exactly the same distances from us, and could have no basic energy source we do not have. That is guaranteed by the common physical and chemical structure of the universe. It is therefore just as difficult for them to visit us, or send instrument-probes in our direction, as it is for us to do this with regard to them. Put quite brutally, it is going to be by electromagnetic communication that we shall learn of each other's existence or not at all.

The first difficulty arising from this situation is that since all communication is a two-way affair, contacts between intelligent extraterrestrials in different stellar *loci* is limited to those having achieved a certain level of scientific awareness and technological ability. This automatically reduces our chances of confirming the hypothesis by one-half. For as I said earlier we can only assume our own level of awareness and technology is the norm. In the absence of a galactic survey, and unless someone can show why our development should be particularly rapid or retarded, we can assume nothing else. Yet we are only at the borderline in these respects. Our scientists have become aware of these possibilities within the past few years merely. We have made only one effort to listen for signals (for three months in 1960, and directed at two very near stars);[13] and of course if one doesn't listen one hears absolutely nothing. Thus all intelligent extraterrestrials below our own stage are below the threshold of knowledge essential for interstellar communication. They are not candidates for confirmation of the hypothesis yet, even if they happen to be quite intelligent and possessed of a rich culture, like medieval Europe's. Indeed, until they reach that threshold, they are completely cut off from contact with intelligent beings in other planetary systems.

But this difficulty is double-edged. For if we are only at the threshold of interstellar communication it seems likely many extraterrestrials passed it long ago. For example, radiocommunication on Earth goes back but fifty years into our history. It is estimated that within another fifty years we shall achieve 'technical perfection' in radiocommunication: i.e. a state where effective communication is no longer limited by deficiencies in the apparatus (such as receiver noise), but only by uncontrollable natural phenomena.[14] Now a century is a very thin slice of Man's history, and of course but a flick of the cosmic eye-lash. That stage in our own technological development could have been completed centuries or even millenniums ago elsewhere. Thus there could be galactic neighbours of ours able to transmit, as Purcell suggests, 10 Mw as easily as we transmit one kilowatt. Several hundred potential sites of extraterrestrial intelligence within 100 light years' distance therefore gives us, even when halved, a lot of hopeful sources to listen to.

The second difficulty follows neatly on the first. Exactly how are we to listen, and for what? And even if we do hear something, what assurance have we that it could be identified as a message from intelligent extraterrestrials?

All these questions have answers, though not everyone is agreed on the right answers. As for how we are to listen, the overwhelming view favours refinement of and extension of current techniques in radioastronomy. (There is a minority interest in optical masers, but largely as a complementary method.) Here the problem involves the relation between bandwidth and frequency. A powerful signal of broad bandwidth is easy to locate because it is spread over a wide frequency-range. But a signal from a distant star, even if very strong upon emission, is bound to be quite feeble upon arrival. It is subject to the same law applying to any form of electromagnetic radiation: namely that its intensity decreases according to the square of the distance from its source. The narrower the bandwidth, then, the more audible a signal will be above background noise. But in that case interstellar communication will be restricted to extremely narrow bandwidths, which makes it just that more unlikely that one will hit upon the right frequency. As has been suggested, searching for interstellar signals by merely scanning frequencies would be like trying to meet a friend in a large city without having agreed on a meeting-place. The logical alternative to just wandering the streets aimlessly would be to try to decide on the most obvious places to meet and hope your friend will have thought of that too. These will be well-known central points in the city, such as a principal railway station, park, famous building, or monument. In 1959 Giuseppe Cocconi and Phillip Morrison suggested what that 'place' would be in terms of interstellar radio communication: the 'Hydrogen Line' at 1420 Mc/sec. (or 21-cm).[15] This is the frequency at which clouds of individual hydrogen atoms in space give off, upon collision, a radio wave that is characteristic and would be detectable through the planetary atmosphere by radioastronomers anywhere in the whole universe. It has subsequently been suggested by others that while this would be the most obvious frequency, observers everywhere would realise detecting it is made difficult by its competition with normal hydrogen emissions of the same wave-length. So they have thought of halving the frequency, or trying multiples of it. But, whichever is the best choice, we are not reduced to scanning the radio spectrum haphazardly, and that in itself affords genuine hope of making successful contacts.

The content of signals received from intelligent extraterrestrials actually presents less of a problem than receiving them. As Cocconi and Morrison point out, the opening of the message would be some attention-getting device. A sequence of pulses representing the small prime numbers, for example, would be unmistakably artificial in origin. Subsequent parts of the message would yield familiar information, such as equations representing physical laws that obtain everywhere in the universe; or formulae representing compounds known to all inorganic chemists. From these it would move on to presumably unfamiliar data, such as descriptions of organic compounds on the home-planet. Decoding such messages involves the same procedures present-day cryptographers employ; all the senders have to do is provide us with the key to the code in its early part. Some simple geometric pattern with an algebraic clue would allow us to make out their scanning raster in a TV-type code.[16]

Our third difficulty in relying entirely upon electromagnetic signalling as a means of confirming the existence of extraterrestrial intelligence is, I am afraid, much more fundamental. This is the problem of knowing how far such beings really are from us. For as we shall see in a moment, the actual distance separating us from other advanced technological societies in the galaxy drastically affects our chances of contacting them by electromagnetic communication. But this is precisely the point on which scientific partisans of the hypothesis are most uncertain. The probability, in a somewhat vague sense of that word, of planetary systems with broad 'habitable' temperature zones and ample time for the emergence of intelligent life, is agreed upon. Beyond that, however, we have no further data which can establish the true frequency of occurrence of intelligent and 'communicable' life in our galactic vicinity. If this is really very frequent, then there might be technologically advanced societies within a radius of only 20 light years which we could certainly hope to contact before too long. But if, due to imponderable factors I shall not discuss here, these occur only rarely, then the nearest may be hundreds or even thousands of light years distant. I repeat that no one can show why the former and not the latter must be the truer case. And, if so, it is perfectly consistent with all we now know that no contact shall be made in the indefinite future.

This can be seen by supposing, for the sake of the argument, that in fact advanced technological societies are situated at about 1000 light years from each other. Not knowing this, we make preparations for receiving signals from near-by stellar sources: say those few likely candidates within 20 light years of us. We build much larger parabolic radiowave reflectors than those we now have, with antenna dishes as wide as 2000 feet, and devote fifty years to listening for contact signals. This fifty-year figure is not arbitrary. Our advanced galactic neighbours are not going to beam signals at us continually; if their first signals do not provoke a reply within that time they will assume we are not yet of age technologically – as indeed we have not been during the past six or seven millenniums of our civilised history. There is no point to their beaming very long messages at us until they get an initial response, and that would take up to fifty years at this range. Now of course if this is what we start by doing, no signals will be detected except by the sheerest chance. For our nearest stellar source of signals is really 1000 light years away. Suppose we then decide we have been too optimistic and begin pointing our radio telescopes at promising stars up to 100 light years away. This time we wait two centures at least, for the same reason given above. Again nothing is heard. But we are persevering, so we now direct our receivers at likely stars up to 1000 light years from us. Should we not be successful now? That is just my point. While the farther out we listen the greater our chances of hitting the right star, the less our chances of actually getting signals from it. For within this radius there are so many stars of the likely sort that the transmitting society, assuming a reasonably limited number of transmitters reserved exclusively for this purpose and a sufficiently narrow emission bandwidth to scan each stellar candidate individually, would need nearly three centuries to beam signals at each one for *one day*.[17] Thus unless we had our receivers directed towards that star on the same day it beamed at us we should still hear nothing, and not have another chance for another 300 years.

Of course there are other possibilities, and we should look briefly at these now. It might occur to us, for example, that our galactic neighbours possessed of advanced technologies are not only far away, but doing the same as we, i.e. just listening, in which case no one will hear anything. So we decide to build transmitters of our own (actually, we should probably want to do that anyway, in order to reply quickly to any signals we receive). This is by no means a light undertaking. A receiving planet the size of the Earth would have to get the signal with a power of 10w if it is to be intelligible and differentiated from cosmic noise. But to direct a signal which arrives with this much power at an Earth-sized planet around even the nearest stars requires either a far greater precision in transmitting instruments, or conversely an enormously greater transmitting power, than we now possess. It is the same problem we saw before: the need for an extremely narrow bandwidth to reduce the energy requirements of transmission where signals lose intensity according to the square of the distance covered. We are not likely to achieve such precision, or such compensating power, within much less than a hundred years. Yet the nearest receiver, I have suggested, might be not 4.5 but 1000 light years' away. This gives one some idea of how far we have to go to be able to contact that galactic neighbour by transmission in terms of our own technological future. But the situation is worse than that. Suppose we decide to install a fixed parabolic transmitter, thereby sweeping the heavens with the rotation of our Earth and hoping to pick up a receiver 'somewhere'. But even at 5 light years' distance such a 'search ray' would go through a planetary system like ours in one second: far too short a time to detect any intentional pulse pattern in the signals.[18] At 1000 light years, of course, it would be utterly hopeless. So we should be reduced to scanning all likely stars within that radius for almost 300 years, hoping the planetary inhabitants near the right star would have their receivers pointing in our direction the day we beamed signals at them. It is perhaps unnecessary to add that even if our first day's effort was successful, we could not know it for 2000 years.

The remaining ways of confirming belief in extraterrestrial intelligence, should the nearest advanced technological society be 1000 light years from us, involve either undiscovered signalling devices or what might be called 'magnaphysics'. There has been talk, for example, of discovering a decade from now some undetermined waves which we should then see to be the 'uniquely rational' method of signalling, superior to the 21-centimetre line or multiples of it. If so, that would reduce our chances of listening for the wrong frequency, or beaming the wrong wave-length, but it eliminates none of the other difficulties I have discussed. It has also been suggested that neutrinos might be used as message carriers, though how this would make signals easier to detect is far from clear: at present we cannot detect any reaching us from space. 'Magnaphysical' proposals include enclosing one's own sun in a cloud of material that absorbs unusual wave-lengths of light, or with particles that cut off some of its light and can be manipulated to form signals, or with a 'shell' of particles that causes it to radiate entirely in the infra-red part of the spectrum. All of these ideas are perhaps feasible, but not for us to undertake in the determinate technological future. Of course if a much farther advanced technological society has already undertaken something like this long before, that would make it possible for us to confirm our hypothesis any day by astronomical observation. It is reported that the Soviet astronomer Shklovskiy recommends studying the Great Spiral Nebula in Andromeda for such signs, since that galaxy can be encompassed within the field of view of a single radio telescope.[19] He admits, however, that to produce a beacon perceptible at that distance the signallers would need to allocate up to 2 per cent of their solar energy for this purpose. They would also have to direct it towards our galaxy, not another. But even if one accepts this as a source of hope, one is reminded that successful detection of such a beacon would tell us no more than this: that two million years ago intelligent extraterrestrials definitely existed. Their contemporary existence could certainly be doubtful over such a great time-span, as pointed out in Case II above. And, as also indicated in my treatment of Case II, any hope of confirming the hypothesis at this distance must be dimmed somewhat by the realisation that two million years ago Man did not even exist, let alone have a technology. Within our own galaxy, of course, and particularly at a mere 1000 light years' distance, these considerations do not apply. But in that case we have our detection problem again, with at least a hundred thousand stellar candidates (some would say as many as a million) spread all over the sky.

There is one further proposal worth mentioning, namely the possibility of 'interstellar eavesdropping': i.e. listening for microwave emissions characteristic of technological civilisations in our galactic vicinity.[20] This is technically interesting and has the advantage of making us independent of intentional signalling in the detection of intelligent extraterrestrial life. However I shall not discuss that possibility here, because even under optimum conditions there is little chance of hearing anything beyond 100 light years away.[21]

I come back now to my main point, that it is perfectly consistent with all we know to suppose the nearest advanced technological society 1000 light years from us, and that in such a case we shall have little chance of contacting one within the foreseeable technological future. But, if so, what then is the logical status of belief in extraterrestrial intelligence?

Two things need to be noted here. First, it is clear from the foregoing discussion that failure to confirm the hypothesis of extraterrestrial intelligence would not by itself invalidate it. Partisans of this view could always point to the scientific 'substructure' – developments in biochemistry and astrophysical theory – to justify their belief and insist we may yet get a confirmation. And since it follows from what I said earlier that it is equally likely there should be advanced technological societies within 20 or so light years' distance as 1000, no one could say the hypothesis had been 'tested' until really extensive efforts were made to find them. Second, this confirmability 'in principle' is not of the vacuous sort mentioned before, since it makes feasible a confirmation in practice under certain conditions, even if we are a long way from establishing those conditions in the technical sense. Nevertheless it is also true that confirmability in principle could become rather vacuous if really sustained efforts produced no result. The hypothesis would gradually lose scientific interest, though not scientific respectability.

This last point has special relevance to our problem. Suppose we did all the things discussed above to confirm the existence of intelligent extraterrestrials, over a period of ten millenniums, but failed to make any contact at all. All this would prove is that advanced technological communities are sparser than we thought in our corner of the galaxy. It would not prove there are none, much less that there are no intelligent extraterrestrials around. What we already know and understand, referring again to the scientific substructure of this hypothesis, gives it a plausibility which could be subverted only by an attack on the substructure itself. Not that this substructure is complete. There are still gaps in the evidence: biochemists have yet to achieve, for example, the formation of replicating polymers under experimental conditions.* And it could be discovered that for some at present quite unspecifiable reason planetary systems are after all very rare. But so long as the substructure remains intact – of course we expect more than that, we expect it to grow more solid and extensive – it will never be idle speculation to assert the existence of intelligent beings in our galactic vicinity.

So much for testability in the sense of possible confirmation. We must now consider what appears a far more serious peculiarity of the hypothesis. You will recall that I said earlier the hypothesis of extraterrestrial intelligence was not testable at all in one important respect, even on the most optimistic assumptions. What I meant, of course, is that there is simply no way to *falsify* it. One can conceivably falsify the scientific substructure – as I just admitted – which would undermine the hypothesis completely. But this is not quite the same thing. Falsification of the hypothesis itself requires actually inspecting all stellar candidates to make sure they either have no planets or, if they have, that those planets are devoid of intelligent life. This you cannot do by electromagnetic signalling for, as we noted before, only half the communities of intelligent extraterrestrials can be expected to have advanced technologies. That means you have to go there and look, or at least send instrument-probes out to look for you. And we have already seen how difficult that would be, even with regard to our immediate solar neighbourhood. How could we ever expect to visit hundreds of sun-like stars within a 100-light-year radius, or a hundred thousand out to 1000 light years? But even then we should not be done. There are at least one hundred million candidates in our galaxy alone, and ten thousand million more known galaxies. But this is probably only one-tenth of the total

*As this book goes to press it has been announced that Dr Arthur Kornberg and his associates at Stanford University, California, have succeeded in synthesising a molecule of DNA in virus form, which, when placed with a host bacteria, became fully active biologically and is indeed self-replicating. (*See* report in *Proc. Nat. Acad. Sci.*, December 1967, Washington, D.C.).

in the universe: beyond what we can see there will be galaxies receding from us at near the speed of light, so that by no stretch of the imagination could we ever catch up to them. Our hypothesis, in other words, is unfalsifiable in principle.

One is uncomfortably aware, at this point, of a *prima facie* similarity between the belief in extraterrestrial intelligence and a notoriously unscientific belief: I mean the belief in an after-life. For in both cases they are open to some sort of confirmability, but remain unfalsifiable even in principle. However, this is a deceptive similarity. Belief in extraterrestrial intelligence is confirmable, if at all, in *this* life; and has, as we saw, a scientific substructure which is itself falsifiable. Nevertheless it remains true that the hypothesis taken alone is strictly unfalsifiable. Partisans of the falsifiability criterion as a means of demarcating scientific from other types of statements may thus feel constrained to assign it a metaphysical or other unflattering logical status. In my concluding remark on this problem I want to face up to that difficulty.

There are two ways, I think, to do so. The first is to counter-attack as follows. 'It must be possible for an empirical scientific system to be refuted by experience', says Popper,[22] and his disciples have concurred in this stand.[23] We have seen this to be true of the scientific substructure of our hypothesis, but if the 'system' includes the assertion of the existence of extraterrestrial intelligent life, then it cannot by this standard qualify as empirical and scientific. Yet at Green Bank, West Virginia, in the summer of 1960 some quite serious radioastronomers were listening for signals at 1420 Mc in the direction of Tau Ceti and Epsilon Eridani. They did not have much hope of hearing anything, but what they were listening for was certainly empirical, and their reasons for doing so were surely scientific. Thus if one insists on a strict interpretation of the falsifiability criterion it can always be answered that this recommended demarcation line is inadequate to describe the range of scientific hypotheses. The second way to handle the difficulty is perhaps more pleasing to everyone concerned. We can treat the statement that intelligent extra-terrestrials exist as an extrapolation, merely, from certain discoveries and theoretical advances in biochemistry and astrophysics. This accords well with the way scientists discuss the hypothesis themselves, and does not involve a direct confrontation with the falsifiability criterion. For my part I shall rest content with the observation that belief in extraterrestrial intelligence has acquired a scientific basis in our time; so that its logical status, while still speculative, is no longer on a par with metaphysical and religious beliefs.

1. See Melvin Calvin's Condon Lecture, 'Chemical Evolution', reprinted as chapter 5 in *Interstellar Communication*, ed. A.G.W.Cameron (Benjamin, N.Y., 1963).

2. Ibid. pp. 68–71.

3. See A.G.W.Cameron, *The Origin of the Solar System*, reprinted in *Interstellar Communication*, ed. Cameron, as chapter 3.

4. Harlow Shapley, *The View from a Distant Star* (Basic Books, N.Y., 1963) ch. 5. In an earlier book, *Of Stars and Men* (Elek, 1958), Shapley used the 'only one in a thousand' formula with, of course, far more conservative results if one preserves the same sequence of steps.

5. See Su-Shu Huang's papers, 'Occurrence of Life in the Universe', 'The Problem of Life in the Universe and the Mode of Star Formation', and 'The Sizes of Habitable Planets', reprinted in *Interstellar Communication*, ed. Cameron, as chapters 6, 7, and 9.

6. A.G.W.Cameron thinks all single stars have planetary systems of some sort, and that the velocity of axial radiation of such stars is irrelevant. See *Interstellar Communication*, p. 29.

7. See Harlow Shapley, *Crusted Stars and Self-Heating Planets* (Tucumán National University, Argentina, 1962: *Mathematica y Fisica Teorica*, Serie A, XIV).

8. See report on Harrison Brown's calculations in *Science News Letter*, 86:199, for 26 September 1964.

9. See Su-Shu Huang in op. cit. pp. 90–1. This conclusion was first reached by Struve in 1952.

10. See 'Radioastronomy and Communication Through Space', Brookhaven

Lecture Series, no. 1, reprinted in *Interstellar Communication*, ed. Cameron, as chapter 13.

11. See his paper, 'The General Limits of Space Travel', reprinted in *Interstellar Communication*, ed. Cameron, as chapter 14.

12. See John W. Macvey, *Journey to Alpha Centauri* (Macmillan Co., N.Y., 1965) especially chapter 12.

13. See Frank Drake, 'Project Ozma', reprinted in *Interstellar Communication*, ed. Cameron, as chapter 17.

14. See Frank Drake, 'How Can We Detect Radio Transmissions from Distant Planetary Systems?', reprinted in *Interstellar Communication*, ed. Cameron, as chapter 16.

15. See their paper, 'Searching for Interstellar Communications', reprinted in *Interstellar Communication*, ed. Cameron, as chapter 15.

16. See Phillip Morrison, 'Interstellar Communication', reprinted in *Interstellar Communication*, ed. Cameron, as chapter 26, pp. 267–70 especially.

17. See Su-Shu Huang, 'Problem of Transmission in Interstellar Communication', reprinted in *Interstellar Communication*, ed. Cameron, as chapter 21, pp. 203–5 especially.

18. See Gösta Ehrensvärd, *Man on Another World* (University of Chicago Press, 1965) pp. 127–30.

19. See Walter Sullivan, *We Are Not Alone: the Search for Intelligent Life on Other Worlds* (McGraw-Hill, 1964) p. 223.

20. See J. A. Webb, 'Detection of Intelligent Signals from Space', reprinted in *Interstellar Communication*, ed. Cameron, as chapter 18.

21. See Webb, op. cit. p. 190. Others think we could detect artificial transmissions out to several thousand light years by this means. Even if we could, it would still be necessary to 'eavesdrop' by intentional *listening* in the direction of each stellar candidate, which presents the same scanning problem on our side.

22. *The Logic of Scientific Discovery* (Hutchinson, 1956) p. 41.

23. Cf. J. W. N. Watkins, 'When are Statements Empirical?', in *British Journal for the Philosophy of Science*, x (1960) 287–308.

N.B. For a much fuller treatment of the matters dealt with here and, to a lesser extent, in the next chapter, see *Intelligent Life in the Universe*, by I. S. Shklovskii (spelt Shklovskiy in other English renditions of the name, and also in the present work) and Carl Sagan (Holden-Day, 1966), particularly chapters 1–30. Chapters 31–35 of this book are, in my view, highly unreliable in their speculative conclusions. The essential scientific work upon which the book is based is that I have drawn upon in these two chapters.

4 *Extraterrestrial Persons: II*

THROUGHOUT the preceding chapter I made various assumptions central to its conclusions. For example, it was assumed without argument that life will evolve into intelligent forms on extrasolar planetary surfaces under certain conditions; that intelligent organisms everywhere tend to develop science and technology; and that a community of technologically advanced beings will have a sustained interest in interstellar communication. My excuse for deferring discussion of these assumptions until now is that they bear directly on the question of the claim intelligent extraterrestrials would have to person-status, and what kind of relations we might possibly have with them. Nevertheless it must be recognised that unless I can justify those assumptions even my conservative conclusions on the prospects for confirming belief in extraterrestrial intelligence would be unwarranted. This is what I meant by unavoidable overlapping between the previous chapter and the present one.

Before taking up the issue of intelligence in extraterrestrial organisms it will be well to consider what one can surmise of the structure and constitution of living things anywhere in the universe.

At first sight this seems of almost unlimited variability from the familiar. It has been suggested, for example, that extraterrestrial life might depend on the chemistry of the silicon atom rather than the carbon atom, which would yield some very exotic results: silicon-based organisms would, for instance, breathe out silicon dioxide (sand) instead of carbon dioxide.[1] Similarly, it has been said that advanced extraterrestrial life might have a metabolism based on hydrogen rather than oxygen, especially if it developed on the surface of a large planet such as Jupiter or Saturn, where high gravity could be expected to retain great quantities of this gas in the primitive atmosphere.[2] However, there is little evidence to support these conjectures. Silicon polymers of the protein type are labile in any known medium, hence unlikely to form the compounds essential for chemical evolution.[3] Planets of the size of Jupiter or Saturn are almost certainly devoid of a water-covered surface, and this seems today absolutely essential as a medium for the emergence of life-systems.[4] Indeed the overwhelming weight of contemporary evidence is on the side of carbon compounds forming in water and nothing else. That is encouraging in one sense: for carbon is most common in the universe. In another sense it is interestingly limitative, for it restricts the evolution of macrorganisms to planets having surface temperatures similar to the Earth's. Thus we may expect that in the neighbourhood of any sun-like star there will only be one or two planets capable of evolving intelligent life.

Into what forms would it evolve? Again one is tempted to suppose there must be enormous variations open to chance evolution. For even if life starts everywhere with carbon compounds in a water medium, there need be only slightly different environmental conditions – which one would certainly expect on distinct planetary surfaces – to produce widely divergent evolutionary trends. Thus one writer says intelligent beings on extrasolar planets might be insect-like, bird-like, fish-like, or even plant-like.[5] Another says that for all we know intelligent extraterrestrials could be spherical in shape: round balls that ingurgitate objects and manipulate them internally the way we manipulate things with our tongues.[6] There is a certain appeal to this conceptual latitutde. After all, the more we learn of nature the more fantastic it seems, and we want at any cost to avoid being anthropomorphic.

Nevertheless our own planet affords some instructive lessons about evolutionary development, lessons which militate strongly against this sort of biological liberalism. One way to approach the point I want to make here, though admittedly indirect, is to consider why we do not believe in the existence – past or present – of certain mythological creatures. It is not just that they figure in myths, nor that we have not personally encountered any, but also because they make no evolutionary sense. Take the centaur, for example. It is conceived to possess the head, trunk, and arms of a man joined to the quadripedal body of a horse. Leaving aside the question of evolving a human brain in a foraging field animal, let us concentrate on the arms. Arms are developed by climbing trees and swinging from branches, which is a little difficult to imagine in conjunction with a horse's body. Such an evolutionary trend was certainly doomed to failure: either the upper part would never develop or the lower would disappear. Or take the griffin, which was supposed to have the head and wings of an eagle joined to the body and hindquarters of a lion. It would be amusing to calculate the spread of wings necessary to make a lion's body fly. It is even more amusing to picture this creature flying, with the soft-spined heavy hindquarters hanging down and contributing nothing to the flight. But suppose it never flew. Then what would it be doing with those enormous wings, which could only impede its attempts to spring on prey? It is because the ancient Greeks knew nothing, or almost nothing, of evolution that they could believe in the existence of such fabulous organisms.

The same kind of point can be made in respect of intelligent extraterrestrials supposed to vary enormously from humans. I shall have occasion later on in this discussion to insist on their not being really like us in other ways, but here I want to argue that from an evolutionary point of view the differences will be relatively negligible. That is to say they will not be like insects, birds, fish, or plants; and they will not be ingurgitating spheres or some other imaginative construction. The heart of my argument –

by no means original[7] – rests on the fact of convergent evolution in plants and animals here on the Earth's surface; and on the not unreasonable, in my view, supposition that a similar convergence will occur in any other planetary environment capable of supporting complex life-systems.

Robert Bieri has presented this argument in a very compact form as follows.[8] Beginning with abiogenetically produced organic matter based on carbon compounds in a water medium, we have a very long period in which herbivores and carnivores reach an advanced level of complexity and specialisation in the oceanic environment, prior to invasion of the land. What characterises most of these animals is bilateral symmetry in the shape of the body. This is not an evolutionary accident of some kind. Such a shape is essential to speed of movement in pursuit and escape in a viscous medium: it is the only shape which reduces water resistance and turbulence to a minimum. The fact that creatures as diverse as the squid and the penguin, as well as the seal and otter and large fish, have this streamlining is itself an important instance of convergent evolution. By contrast, when bilaterally symmetrical ocean-dwellers adopt a relatively stationary way of life, they lose it and take on radial symmetry, with an accompanying loss of sensitivity and degeneration of the nervous system. Animals with primal radial symmetry, i.e. whose ancestors never had bilateral symmetry, exhibit a uniformly low level of organisation. Thus it is clear that evolution of a complex nervous system is contingent upon adoption of the active, predatory way of life.

Now it is equally significant, Bieri argues, that predatory animals with complex nervous systems and a bilaterally symmetrical shape have an anterior mouth and posterior anus. Again this is no chance development. With few exceptions it is characteristic of all predators. The reason is again simple: this is obviously the best method of ingestion and excretion for an active hunting animal. Similarly, it is the case that almost without exception the leading surface of the predator contains its largest and most important sensing and grasping organs, in close proximity to the mouth it must feed. Nor is it strange that the largest ganglion of nerves, or brain as the case may be, is located in the same area. This reduces the time it takes to send nerve impulses from the sensing organs to the nerve centre and back to the grasping organs, and it provides better protection to the nerve centre from attack or damage. Even in highly efficient two-directional creatures such as the squid major sense organs are grouped at one end of the body near the brain and mouth. As Bieri says, these elements of the organism do not migrate to distant parts of the body, no matter what its particular evolutionary antecedents. Such features are so widespread among predatory animals that they cannot be supposed to result from some accident in the dim past, only one of many possibilities. They have evolved independently in group after group, again and again.

Thus we may be reasonably certain that advanced organisms emerging from a liquid environment will be bilaterally sym-metrical with a large ganglion of nerves, or brain, at the front end and near the mouth and principal sense organs. Once the transfer to land surfaces becomes permanent there should occur consider-able growth and refinement of both nerve tissues and the integrating nerve-centre, leading eventually to conceptualisation. Why this is more likely to take place among land animals than sea-dwellers or birds is easy to see. It is true that dolphins provide an example of large-scale brain development in an aquatic medium, but conceptualisation seems to arise in conjunction with a social existence, speech, and the use of tools. Bieri points out that development of tools in a liquid medium is highly improb-able, given the density and viscosity of water. The sea otter, for example, rises to the surface to break up food on his chest. Use of even such a simple tool as a lever is difficult under water; and the projection of objects as weapons practically impossible. Besides, sound waves are much more easily distorted in a liquid than in a gas, especially if the liquid is in constant motion as the sea is.[9] It is therefore extremely unlikely that a brain capable of conceptual thought, which presupposes a social environment and some form of objective language, will develop under these conditions. As for birds, the limitations are even more severe. If it is to fly it must be light in weight with a large surface area: hollow bones in birds are a good example of the necessary adjustments it must make. But a large brain requires a large supply of blood, a large heart to pump it in quantity. This is just what a bird cannot afford if it is to pursue and elude things through the air.[10] Thus we have narrowed the feasible evolutionary routes down to this: a predatory land animal with the basic structure described above, able to manipulate tools, live in groups, and communicate by sound-waves through air.

But even that rough description leads on to a more detailed one. How will the land predator move about? Sliding on slime limits it to riverbanks, swamps, etc. Wriggling is painfully slow. Bieri points out that wheels have never been evolved in a living organism: tissues cannot sustain the high pressures a wheel bearing undergoes, and in any case you need flat land for wheels. Walking seems the only viable alternative, for by walking you can go over all kinds of terrain, quickly when necessary, and carrying with you a large brain well supplied with blood. So legs will be required, and for maximum efficiency they must be jointed legs as well. Berrill reminds us that even then two kinds of legs are possible. You can have hard levers and struts surrounded by muscles and tendons, as in land-walking vertebrates; or you can have the reverse arrangement, hollow cylinders with muscles and tendons inside the skeletal tube, as is the case with insects and other creatures. However, the additional strength and lightness secured by the latter relationship is outweighed by the restrictions it imposes on increase of size: one of the reasons why insects remain relatively small.[11] How many legs are likely? One won't do: how would the fallen creature get back up quickly? Odd-numbered appendages are quite rare, probably because of the balance problem. How many pairs then? Large numbers of paired appendages are suitable for slow-moving creatures like the millipede, but not for predators. A single body so propelled flows along, each short leg swinging through its brief arc quickly and in succession; longer legs would get in each other's way, yet long legs are just what is needed for ground clearance and spring.[12] In fact the fossil record shows a progressive reduction of paired appendages, until we get the insect with three pairs in the middle section, able to scuttle and pounce very quickly indeed. Bieri suggests that six legs for insects may be due to their small size and exoskeleton of chitin, while the four characteristic of vertebrates may be traced back to their aquatic origins and the need for stabilising and steering appendages in speed swimming.[13] In any case the successful land predator ought to have not less than two and not more than three pairs of appendages anywhere that conditions allow his evolution. Two seems the more promising for development of a large brain because this facilitates conversion of one pair to arms through arboreal ascent, and makes tool-manipulation easier in the post-arboreal phase.

Must we stop there? How about sense organs? Once more there is a *prima facie* case for wide variation from the familiar. Why could not intelligent organisms have entirely distinct senses, so distinct we cannot even imagine what they are like? If they did this would constitute a formidable limitation on potential information-exchanges with them: we should be reduced to transmitting only that data which is quantitatively expressible. Fortunately, the principle of convergent evolution is applicable here too. We have to start with a physical environment which cannot, as we have seen, differ greatly from the Earth's. Then we may ask what kinds of sense organs would have survival value for land predators in that environment.

Certainly a sense of vision would be valuable on any planetary surface where light radiated from the central star strikes objects and is reflected from them. As Berrill points out, one of the most curious parallels in our animal world is the similarity of eye-structure between such completely unrelated creatures as, for example, advanced octopus-like molluscs and vertebrates. Each type has independently evolved the perfect camera-like eye complete with lens, retina, focusing muscles, transparent cornea, etc.[14] There is a convergence also with regard to the number and position of eyes. One eye is rare, usually serving only to help the organism move towards or away from a source of light. Multiple eyes, as in the case of the spider, work all right if they function in succession, but are individually of an inferior sort compared to the camera-type eye. With the latter only two are needed for stereo-scopic and depth vision: more than that confuses the animal. The position of such eyes is of course in the head near the nerve-centre and grasping organs; and in land predators as high in the body as possible for seeing over obstacles and at a distance. Similar principles apply to the other senses. There is an obvious advantage in being able to detect pressure changes impinging on one's body, which in the case of land animals and birds leads to evolution of hearing devices. Again binaural hearing is best. Two ears are needed for locating the source of sounds, while more than two causes confused perceptions. For the same reason as given above, they will be placed high in the body and near the brain. Similarly with sensors to detect chemicals in solution or dispersed in the air: taste and smell. Only one mouth is needed, with taste sensors distributed along its inner surfaces; the smell sensors are best located very near the mouth, in order to test the edibility of materials about to enter it.[15] Tactile sensors spread all over the body surface are so common to all organisms that they require no special mention here. Bieri grants that additional sense organs are possible, such as infrared detectors for night vision or an acoustical ranging system like that of bats; but as he says these imply a corresponding reduction of vision in the ultraviolet spectrum, which would impede the evolution of tools and associated development of a large brain.[16]

When we set down all these considerations two major conclusions emerge with, I think, great force. The first relates directly to one of the assumptions I made in the previous chapter: namely that under certain conditions life-systems will evolve into intelligent forms on extrasolar planetary surfaces. That assumption has been challenged by eminent biologists[17] on the grounds that life can evolve in an unlimited number of directions and thus the likelihood of it evolving into organisms with a nervous system like ours is extremely small. If so, it follows that our chances of communicating with other intelligent beings in the galactic vicinity would be practically nil. Against this pessimistic view we can now formulate a firm stand. Given an Earth-like environment, life will arise spontaneously and take a number of diverse forms in a liquid medium. Among those some, like the Cetacea, will become fast-swimming predators with a highly organised nervous system and definite pattern of responses to stimuli which can only be termed 'intelligent'. Some will migrate to and populate land surfaces, where the development of speech, manipulation of tools, and adoption of a social form of existence becomes possible. For these types of animals there is no question but that intelligence has enormous survival value. It is of course true that for a great number of other kinds of organisms survival is possible without intelligence: one has only to look at the insects to see this. But once vertebrate land predators appear, intelligence confers great advantages upon them. The virtual conquest of all other such species by *Homo sapiens* on this planet and his unopposed proliferation throughout the extremes of the terrestrial environment amply attest to this fact. It can still be only a matter of conjecture why this single species proved so successful against its ancient rivals in the biosphere. Probably the following factors were all crucial: a long life-span and gestation-period, a slow-forming highly convoluted brain, the evolution of arms and dactyls through arboreal ascent, later permitting the use of tools and weapons, and a protracted period of parental dependence during which a social mode of life was necessary, giving rise therefore to symbolic speech as a means of storing and transmitting collective knowledge of the environment. The same route of evolution would be open, therefore, to at least one species of land predators on every planet where they could be expected to abound. No one can say how often this has actually occurred in extrasolar planetary systems: that is one of the sources of uncertainty about the actual distance separating us from 'communicable' societies in the galaxy. But that it has happened frequently enough to justify efforts to contact them is certain. Or, put another way, it is certainly not the case that all such efforts are foredoomed because of any *a priori* probability that intelligent extraterrestrials are very rare in the universe.

My second major conclusion from the foregoing discussion of convergent evolution is simply that intelligent extraterrestrials everywhere will resemble *Homo sapiens* to a considerable extent. This is of course the finding of Bieri, Berrill, and others; it follows inescapably from the fact that here on Earth animals and plants have independently evolved not only similar structures, but also similar biochemical systems and similar behavioural patterns as solutions to the same fundamental problems. To cite just two further examples of this not mentioned before, consider how the gravity-sensitive balancing organ is basically the same in the shrimp, jellyfish, octopus, and almost all vertebrates from fish to man; and how almost all birds and mammals, subjected to rapidly changing temperatures in the surrounding air, have evolved a metabolism allowing them to maintain constant body temperatures. These are not accidental developments, except in the sense that mutations are accidental. They are the simplest solutions available in the physico-chemical environment common to all planetary surfaces on which life-systems can evolve. This is not to say, naturally, that intelligent extraterrestrials will be indistinguishable from humans. Even very light variations in planetary environments are enough to insure significant differences; and there remain relatively unspecialised vertebrate characteristics which can vary from species to species. For example, the structure of tool-manipulating hands could just as easily include three, four, six, or seven fingers: one being an opposing thumb. Less than three seems insufficiently flexible; more than seven is probably cumbersome; but there is no magical quality in the number five. Again, the outer surface of the organism, while probably a hairy skin, could have a different pigmentation or thickness depending on the intensity of solar radiation, etc. On planets slightly larger than the Earth, with correspondingly higher gravity, intelligent beings might be somewhat stunted, with heavy bones and very powerful musculature. One can go on and on, but not endlessly. Claws and tongs are not going to replace fingers: they do not work as well. Feathers or scales are not going to take the place of a skin: not for a land predator. A stunted body is still going to have arms, a head, long digestive tubes coiled into the body, etc. For there is no known way to escape these steps in the evolution of a tool-manipulating, socialising, symbol-using animal. We can confidently leave webbed feet and antennas and built-in microscopes and cubed bodies for the science-fiction writers. As Bieri put the issue, any major modifications in the picture here presented can be seriously considered only when their proponents are able to state a reasonable series of evolutionary steps leading up to the final structures derived. In the absence of that, we may be sure any such beings will look more or less like us.

It is interesting, in my view, that some scientists have gone to the opposite extreme and called intelligent extraterrestrials 'humans'.[18] Now surely they do not mean this in a strict biological sense. As we just saw, there are bound to be variations in secondary features due to slight differences in planetary environments. What is more, a common humanity in the biological sense would mean potential reproduction through sexual intercourse, which is excessively unlikely. Indeed, to be members of the same species biologically involves exact duplication or multiplication of the genetic code on diverse planetary surfaces. The chances of this happening are as great as, say, all intelligent extraterrestrials speaking English. But if writers who talk that way do not mean this, what do they mean? I think it pretty clear they mean no more than that all intelligent, conceptualising organisms are *like* humans in those respects. So much is evident from the quite widespread practice among scientists of referring to intelligent extraterrestrials as 'humanoids', or 'huminoids'.

This is an interesting phenomenon for two reasons. First, because it illustrates the conceptual poverty of scientists and the limited range of human experience underlying it. What I mean is that scientists have had direct experience of only one kind of intelligent, tool-manipulating organism capable of true speech and a truly social form of existence. It is therefore perfectly understandable that they should think of similar organisms as 'human', or at least 'humanoid'. But it is not at all difficult to imagine quite different circumstances in other planetary systems. For example, it could well be that on two, rather than just one, planets of the same system such beings have evolved. In that case they could have had by our present standards of technology not only electromagnetic contacts, but even direct physical confrontation with each other long ago. There would be no question, under such conditions, of one community using its biological designation for the other. They would certainly settle on a logically higher concept which includes both. In fact the same process could conceivably take place much earlier in their evolution: even at a pre-scientific stage. For it is possible a single planet in another system would have widely separated continents, on each of which such organisms evolved independently and then discovered each other the way some human societies discovered each other from the seventeenth to the nineteenth centuries.* Again a higher

* It is of course true that even on Earth at least four distinct 'hominid' populations evolved and came into contact with each other as intelligent organisms. However, this took place not merely in a pre-scientific but also in a

concept would emerge, embracing all the species of this type; not out of any altruistic feelings necessarily, but in order to distinguish themselves collectively from animals not having achieved such a level.

What would be the higher logical concept embracing all organisms of this type? That is the second feature of contemporary scientific provincialism I find interesting. For, as I argued in Chapter 1, the fact is that the logic of our language already allows for a broader concept. If present-day scientists are not aware of this, it is only because they have not – again quite understandably – troubled to analyse our notion of a 'person'. If they did, I think they would find that although human beings are persons, not all persons need be human. To qualify as a person an entity must, as I said, be capable of both these things: the assimilation of a conceptual scheme and the experience of sensations, emotional states, etc. Which is to say that persons are always potential 'moral agents'. I shall have more to say about extraterrestrials *qua* moral agents later on, but for the moment note how intelligent, conceptualising organisms in other planetary systems fulfil both these conditions. Unlike intelligent, even parahuman machines such as those described in Chapter 2, there is no reasonable basis for doubting they have feelings. All their constituent elements are organic, and indeed evolved naturally just the way ours did. Given naturally evolved sensors, glands, nervous systems, and so on, how could we fail to ascribe to extraterrestrial organisms sensations of light, sounds, odours, pains; or feelings of hunger, lust, and anger? Indeed they would in these respects be on a par with the hypothetical organic artifacts discussed at the end of Chapter 2, who are conceived as biologically 'separate,

---

prehistorical period. If they had a higher logical concept embracing each other and distinguishing themselves collectively from lower animals, it did not survive with *Homo sapiens'* emergence into the historical period beginning about 8000 B.C.

but equal'. And like them they should have good reason to resent a proprietary title such as 'humanoid': even more so since their biological parity would owe nothing to human inventiveness.

This brings us to the second major assumption concealed in the previous chapter's discussion. For even if planets are abundant and life widespread in the galaxy, and even if the principles of convergent evolution assure a fundamental biological uniformity between intelligent organisms throughout the galactic vicinity, this affords no certainty that we shall contact them in the foreseeable future. Our hope of doing so must rest on the further supposition that intelligent extraterrestrials are likely to develop science and technology. And here we face the same kinds of difficulties as before. Any justification of this assumption, in other words, will have to involve an extrapolation from human experience. So the question becomes this: is there anything in the historical experience of mankind one can point to as evidence for the probable development of technology and science among extraterrestrial communities? Or is this feature of human history accidental, hence unlikely to be paralleled elsewhere?

Technology considered by itself presents no particular difficulty. For one thing, the beginning of technology is tool-manipulation, which, as we saw, is presupposed in the very evolution of intelligent organisms. And in fact there is a kind of indirect evidence for technological convergence in the history of our own race. Through most of the historical period *Homo sapiens* has lived in relative cultural dispersion on the Earth; some of these isolates, such as the Australian Aborigines, having become known to the rest of us only within the past two centuries. Yet without exception all culture-groups have developed a technology of sorts. Indeed one of the most striking features of anthropology is the fact that men everywhere, even in isolated cultures such as the South American or Chinese, developed much the same artifacts and techniques for controlling their environment. We do not find this surprising because, despite regional differences, it is, after all, basically the same environment. Nor should it be surprising, then, that on other planetary surfaces like the Earth's extraterrestrials will have found similar technological solutions to their problems. That is not to deny the possibility of significant differences. The level of technological development relative to ours will depend, of course, on opportunities afforded by the particular environment and on the time available to exploit them. A planet poor in metals or energy sources, for example, will not allow so high a development as our own. But conversely, technological development would be accelerated on a planet where these things are more abundant or easily accessible than on Earth. As for the time available, one can only repeat what was said in the previous chapter, i.e. that in the absence of a cosmic survey we have to assume our own evolution neither exceptionally quick nor unusually retarded. Thus half the extraterrestrial communities in our galactic vicinity will have technologies at least as advanced as ours, and a great many of these far more advanced ones: we know how much difference a single century can make.

A much stronger case for disparity between ourselves and extraterrestrials can be presented with regard to science. It might be argued that what we call 'modern science', at least, is not a convergent phenomenon in the history of the race, but a cultural development unique to post-Renaissance Europe, only recently adopted by most of the remaining cultures and even then rather reluctantly. And since this development has completely transformed technology, not only quantitatively, but qualitatively, it would seem to follow that very few communities of intelligent extraterrestrial organisms would have a technology equal to or surpassing our own. Against this, however, one can urge the following points. First, the distinction between science and technology is itself highly arbitrary. They are not different 'forms of life', the way religion and economic activity are, but complementary aspects of a single intellectual process directed to the same overall goal of comprehending and controlling the physical environment. Second, and growing out of that observation, it seems likely that if Galileo and his successors had not hit upon the use of mathematical models to describe natural laws, the correct experimental method, etc., someone else certainly would have done so. For this is not at all like saying, for example, that if Shakespeare had not written his plays another person would have written them; the difference being that in the former case all men interested in understanding and ultimately controlling their common physical environment were groping towards the same end. The proper analogy, in other words, is not with individual expressions of artistic genius, but with a team of rivals seeking the true solution to a familiar problem. And finally, the very fact that modern science has become almost universal among diverse human cultures within the past three hundred years is significant. This was surely not an instance merely of 'cultural borrowing', like adopting alien patterns of dress or even art-forms. If anything it underlines the peculiar survival value of scientific techniques to any community of intelligent organisms, and thus constitutes an illustration by derivative convergence of their potential universality. For all these reasons the emergence of what we call modern science among extraterrestrials appears just as likely, on the basis of human experience, as the emergence of technology itself.

But even if we can be reasonably assured on all these points, there remains one problem to which our experience will not be fully relevant because of its incompleteness. I mean the problem arising from my third major assumption, namely that technological civilisations everywhere will have a *sustained* interest in communicating with their galactic confrères.

At the Green Bank Conference[19] on interstellar communication in 1961, and also in independent discussions by scientists since then, this problem was rated the most uncertain yet decisive factor in any estimate of our chances of contacting extraterrestrial civilisations. For if such communities engaged in efforts at interstellar contacts only briefly, then the number of truly 'communicable' societies during any given time-span – say a century – would be small and the distances separating them correspondingly enormous.

Among the scientists concerned with this uncertainty two general hypotheses have been put forward as possible causes of a merely transitory interest in interstellar communication. One is that for unspecified reasons an advanced technological society might turn away from science altogether, and lapse into mysticism or something else. The other is that such a society, though carrying forward its efforts at interstellar communication, might be unable to avoid a planetary catastrophe provoked by the destructive power of the technology which makes such efforts possible. I shall take up these hypotheses in turn.

As for the first, it certainly is true that our own experience has only a limited relevance to the possibility it envisions. We are only on the threshold of interest in interstellar communication. If the difficulties I described in the previous chapter are real ones, we shall need at least another century to make a thorough attempt at contacting extraterrestrials, even within a relatively short radius of light years. And if we were unsuccessful, yet determined to extend our efforts to greater distances, we could very well invest a millennium or two in the search for signals from other civilisations. By that time who can say what cultural transformations our society might have undergone?

Of course no one can. That is the whole point. Where the future of a civilisation is concerned, there is no need to accept a particular possibility unless those urging it can give good reasons for it. Our own experience, admittedly restricted, certainly does not favour this possibility and indeed militates against it. In the three hundred years or so since modern science and technology had their beginnings there is not a single case of a human culture turning away from the new *Weltanschauung* to mysticism, quietism, or what have you.

H

Individuals have done that, as they do in any age, but not a culture-group. All such instances up to the present have involved pre-scientific – in the modern sense – cultures whose technologies were subservient to otherworldly ends: one thinks here of the Ancient Egyptian and Middle American civilisations. Indeed it can be argued that the longer and more widespread a scientific culture the less chance there is of this happening, precisely because such an outlook focuses attention on the physical environment and tends to drive out otherworldly concerns. (Note in this connection how rare it is in the more advanced technological cultures to attribute drought, floods, earthquakes, etc., to super-natural causes.) Of course these considerations cannot rule out the possibility of such a transformation two thousand years from now, but they do make it seem a rather arid conjecture.

The second hypothesis is usually taken far more seriously, and with good reason. It seems no accident of history that at the same time we have become aware of and interested in the possibility of interstellar communication we should also be in danger of destroying the very technology underlying it. Our experience is still, thankfully, incomplete and hence not fully relevant to the problem; but, if anything, it is far more complete than in the former case. What is more, one can argue for a kind of secondary convergence from human experience: namely that a species evolves in isolated culture-groups during its immediate pre-scientific and early historical period; that these culture-groups compete with each other in exploiting environmental opportunities; that the tribes and kingdoms and empires and nation-states they form to this end repeatedly wage war on each other, whether in the service of some spurious ideology or not; and that once some of these groups reach a technological level sufficiently high to use basic energy sources for weapons – what might be called the 'Nuclear Level' – they are then in a position to destroy the civilisation as a whole. All this is amply attested to by our experience: it leads to what some scientists have termed 'the longevity problem in technological civilisations'.

Yet the argument strikes me as narrowly anthropocentric in ways the preceding contentions were not. For while the earlier claims centred on the universal survival value of science and technology and on the unlikelihood of spontaneous abandonment of a scientifically oriented culture, for which there is no precedent in human experience, this argument assumes that our specific political experience will be reproduced elsewhere. Of course it could, but I think the chances that it has been or will be paralleled in other technological civilisations rather small. I am not denying that extraterrestrial organisms would probably evolve in isolated culture-groups during the pre-scientific stage, and certainly not that they would be warlike towards each other: after all, their biological ancestors were land predators too. But that the history of our political institutions should be a convergent phenomenon in the galaxy is another matter. It is perfectly possible that a global community of intelligent organisms achieves political unity before the discovery of what we call modern science and technology.* Some very stable and internally peaceful empires – such as the Roman and the Chinese – illustrate that tendency in our own experience. Why no truly global society emerged in human history is a question that cannot be answered by philosophical generalisation, but only by pointing to the specific historical forces at work: and these are just what we cannot expect to be duplicated elsewhere. Our whole concept of rival states could be buried in the historical memory of most other advanced technologies, for all we know. The very least – and

* Though we have no warrant for believing so. As Professor Flew has pointed out to me in correspondence, it may very well be that the emergence of what we call modern 'nation-states' presupposes an advanced technology. All I want to argue is that we cannot be sure one way or the other, hence cannot blithely make 'civilisation-crisis' a definite factor in computing the galactic population of 'communicable' societies.

perhaps also the most – one can say on this matter is that we have no warrant for postulating a 'civilisation-crisis' among extraterrestrial communities on the basis, merely, of our own.

For similar reasons it seems to me one can have little patience with the view, expressed by some scientists, that one of the primary advantages of establishing contact with other civilisations would be to learn from them how to solve our problems and weather our crises.[20] Undoubtedly the political institutions under which extraterrestrials live are describable in terms familiar to us. But that from their experience some magical notions could be obtained and readily applied to our specific problems presupposes a simplicity in them by no means evident to political scientists. I am afraid that reports of extraterrestrial political structures, while certainly interesting, would be among the least practical items of information we could obtain from other civilisations in the galaxy. The same would be true of their histories. It is only a species of historical romanticism to suppose knowledge of another civilisation's history applicable to one's own difficulties. For history never does 'repeat itself': at least not in sufficiently specific ways to afford the historian means of predicting its course. This should be even more obvious where the historical knowledge concerns a biologically distinct race in another planetary system.

We come back now to the firmer ground of contemplating the nature of intelligent extraterrestrials on the basis of convergent evolution. I have already argued that despite secondary biological differences they would certainly qualify for person-status, since they would be both capable of assimilating a conceptual scheme and the sort of entity to which one can quite reasonably ascribe feelings. Since these are, as we saw earlier in this book, the essential requirements for constituting a moral agent, to say that extraterrestrials are persons is the same as to say they are moral agents. However, it was pointed out in Chapter 1 that such a designation is 'morally neutral' in the sense that from the fact of being a person or moral agent no particular moral attitude follows. The questions I wish to take up next arise from that observation. I want to ask, first, if this moral neutrality makes it impossible to say anything about the moral relations obtaining within a postulated extraterrestrial community; and, second, what implications it has, if any, for possible moral relations between ourselves and extraterrestrial persons.

The foundation for my argument in both these connections is Professor H. L. A. Hart's illuminating discussion of what he calls 'the minimum content of Natural Law'.[21] While rejecting the metaphysical claims underlying classic Natural Law doctrine, Hart does not feel we are thereby constrained to embrace a narrow positivistic view of legal structures. Instead he finds a modest basis for going beyond that in the observation that most men most of the time wish to continue in existence, so that in a sense it is true to say the 'proper end' of human activity is survival. However, this is not put forward as a description of 'human essence' or 'God's design'. It is asserted merely to be a contingent fact, but one from which certain social arrangements follow, without which a social organisation could not be viable. Coupled with this generalised desire for survival are five further facts about the human situation which Hart designates 'simple truisms', and which afford a reason why law and morals should have some specific content rather than just any at all.

The first of these is the fact that men are occasionally prone to, and normally vulnerable to, bodily attack. Though a truism, this is not, Hart points out, a necessary truth. There are species of animals whose physical structure – like the insect's exoskeleton – renders them virtually immune from attack by members of their own species; and others devoid of any attacking organs. If men were constructed this way, there would be little point to the more characteristic provision of law and morals: 'Thou shalt not kill.' Social life for a community of humans would thus be utterly impossible without forbearances, usually formulated negatively as prohibitions, that take into account men's proneness to attacking each other bodily and their vulnerability to its effects. Second is what Hart calls the fact of 'approximate equality', meaning that despite differences in physical strength, agility, and intellectual capacity, no individual human is so much more powerful than others that he is able to dominate or subdue others for very long without co-operation. Thus the only alternative to continuous unrestrained aggression, with everyone suffering its effects from time to time, is a system of mutual forbearance and compromise; this is of course the basis of moral obligation, which eventually leads to organised legal forms restraining those who exploit it by simultaneously living within its shelter and breaking its irksome restrictions. Again, Hart reminds us, things could have been otherwise. There could have arisen a breed of particularly powerful men with much to gain by aggression, hence uninterested in accepting such restraints. Thus the approximate equality of men is a 'natural fact', not a necessary truth. Third, Hart accepts as a contingent fact that men are characterised by 'limited altruism'. They are neither completely motivated by self-interest and aggressive impulses nor entirely loving and considerate of others. If they were the first no moral code or legal institutions could arise; if they were the latter there would be no need for these things. Fourth, it is a contingent fact, merely, that men require food, clothing, shelter; and that the sources of these necessities are limited, making it necessary to cultivate or construct them by labour. Thus some minimal form of property needs to be instituted and recognised. Were humans foraging animals in abundant fields, or able like plants to extract nourishment from the elements without effort, no concept of property would appear. The necessity for co-operative effort and the advantages of a division of labour, moreover, give rise to contracts and obligation-creating rules which would otherwise have no place in human experience. And finally, the fact that men have a limited understanding of their long-term interest in forbearance and compromise, and that they have a limited strength of will to resist satisfying their short-term interest at the expense of others: these contingent realities of human nature require organised coercion in the form of legal sanctions directed at those who will not, or not always, voluntarily submit to a system of mutual forbearances. Voluntary co-operation within a coercive system, Hart says, is what reason demands of beings constituted as men are and situated in the environment they share.

Now it is obvious even from this sketchy presentation that Hart's analysis of the 'minimum content of Natural Law' is applicable to extraterrestrial communities as well. For we have already seen how the principle of convergent evolution assures a considerable uniformity between ourselves and extraterrestrials. They, like us, will be descended from vertebrate land predators: hence prone to and vulnerable to bodily attack. As a biological species distinct from yet akin to *Homo sapiens*, there seems no inherent reason why each such community of extraterrestrials should not be characterised by the 'approximate equality' of its members in strength and intelligence, however great the variations between communities. A parallel 'limited altruism' among them is suggested by their similar biological ancestry on the one hand, and the social existence presumed in achieving conceptualising intelligence on the other. The former guarantees a degree of selfish aggressiveness, as in humans; the latter some understanding of community interests and a measure of concern, perhaps even love, for others, reinforced by a long period of parental dependence. And of course extraterrestrials will not be plant-like, but higher vertebrates: hence they will need food, shelter, and clothing to be won by labour too. Nor is there any reason to doubt they will have only a limited understanding of long-term interests and a limited strength of will to resist temptations. Thus all the same contingent 'natural necessities' remarked by Hart with regard to humans should characterise extraterrestrials. Arising from them, then, will be a system of mutual forbearances rooted in voluntary compliance and supplemented by organised coercion, just as on our own planet. For this reason I think that if we ever establish communications with extraterrestrial societies we shall find their moral concepts and legal structures recognisably familiar, at least in these more fundamental respects.

The question of the sort of moral relations that might eventually obtain between ourselves and extraterrestrials is more complex and speculative. In order to answer it I shall arbitrarily stipulate three distinct situations.

The first situation is where we come into direct physical contact with extraterrestrial persons. The extreme unlikelihood of this occurring will be obvious from my discussion in the previous chapter of time and energy requirements for interstellar travel. Nevertheless there are circumstances under which this could take place in the distant future. I shall outline four possibilities now. (1) Extraterrestrials simply invade our solar system, unannounced, and quickly select Earth as the most suitable planet for their visit. This is the event which many credulous humans imagine has already taken place, or is taking place all the time. However, such a visit would hardly be inspired by the sort of beneficent curiosity described in popular accounts. To come unbidden all that way, without any advance assurance of their reception or even of what they will find, bespeaks a terrible desperation. Nothing less than an impending natural catastrophe would prompt such sacrifice and resolution. Here, I am afraid, we could expect only a brief and violent struggle: they would not come unarmed. (2) Under similar pressures, we invade another planetary system unbidden and unannounced. Exactly the same sort of struggle would surely ensue, for the same reasons. There would simply be no time to establish any kind of patient understanding under such conditions. Invasion of an alien stellar vicinity this way would always be an act of desperate aggression to be resisted by force. (3) and (4) Having established electromagnetic communication with each other over a very long period of time, either we undertake an interstellar voyage to an extraterrestrial community's abode or vice versa. This could be because one society faces annihilation – such as heating up of the parent star or loss of oxygen in the planetary atmosphere – and has been invited to migrate and resettle; or because one such society feels ready to afford the expense and effort this requires out of scientific interest and a spirit of adventure.

What makes such a physical confrontation vaguely plausible is the time factor. I spoke of an impending natural catastrophe. The most likely one is, of course, the heating up of a parent star. Our own sun will surely become a 'red giant' some day: converting all its hydrogen to helium and in the process roasting all the inner planets. But that will not occur before another eight to ten thousand million years have gone by. The same is presumably true of stellar candidates for intelligent life in the galactic vicinity, since these are in a similar evolutionary state. (That is one reason why I think we need not fear invasion by extraterrestrials for a very long time to come.) Given a stable society, we certainly could expect enormous technological progress between now and then. After all, fully 90 per cent of all the professional scientists of our race are alive today, yet science has already transformed our society beyond recognition. We expect, quite rightly, that great advances will be made within the next century alone. Thus it seems not impossible that during a period of a dozen millions of millenniums a space voyage powered by high-energy sources, and taking hundreds or even thousands of years to complete, would be undertaken.

Remote as the possibility may be, it does allow us to conceive of forming a single society with extraterrestrial persons, either here on Earth or on their planetary abode. It is important to note this is conceivable without presupposing *biological* assimilation of one species by another (as in the case of fanciful person-artifacts discussed at the end of Chapter 2, who were pictured to be on biological parity with *Homo sapiens* yet distinct from it). For the same 'natural necessities' would be contingent facts about extraterrestrial persons, I have argued, and this is the basis for a moral code reinforced by legal sanctions. The secondary biological differences between us and them would not prevent formation of a common community of persons living under the same system of mutual forbearances: though relatively minor rules, such as marriage laws, might have varying applicability. In all fundamental respects, at least, social aims could be served by both species despite their biological diversity, particularly since these aims are rooted in a common desire for survival in a similar physical environment. So much seems to follow from the same principle of convergence which leads to the expectation of rough biological uniformity with regard to their evolutionary antecedents. Social assimilation without biological identity as its foundation is thus distinctly possible, even if interstellar distances leave it a quite hypothetical possibility so far as humans are concerned.

The second situation is quite different. Here we succeed in establishing electromagnetic contact with a relatively near-by extraterrestrial community – say at 50 light years' distance – and within a century have completed the first signal exchange. It must not be thought that this is like a telephone conversation with a hundred years' wait before one side can speak again. Immediately after beaming the recognition signal the receiving party begins to send a steady stream of information signals; as these arrive and are decoded the transmitting party beams back relevant information. So that throughout the century of waiting for a counter-response the receiving party is actively transmitting itself, and from that point on is receiving information in a constant stream based on acknowledgement of all it sent out during the intervening century. Obviously two societies 50 light years apart can learn an awful lot about each other over the first two centuries of communication, even though the original transmitting party heard nothing for the first half of that period. But to get back to my point, suppose it becomes clear to both civilisations that neither imagines itself in a position to attempt an interstellar visit in the foreseeable technological future, though the possibility could be realised in some remote contingency millenniums from the present. For all practical purposes they would have to reconcile themselves to permanent physical separation. The question now becomes this: are any kinds of moral relations possible between communities of intelligent organisms separated by such great distances that they have no reasonable expectation of physical confrontation and assimilation into a single society?

The best way to approach this question, I think, lies in asking what motives would prompt them to engage in interstellar communication in the first place. There is, to begin with, the intensely exciting prospect of confirming the existence of other intelligent, conceptualising, and technologically able organisms in the universe. However, we must recognise that this motive could be absent from the extraterrestrials we succeed in contacting. For they could have learned that much, as I suggested earlier, within their own planetary system. Nevertheless it would be a most powerful incentive for human organisms. Next, and more practically, there are the specific scientific and technological benefits to be gained from information exchanges with extra-terrestrials. On the whole it is unlikely this would be so promising to an extraterrestrial civilisation as to us, should our first contact be made within the next century or so. I say this because, as I pointed out in the previous chapter, we are only on the threshold of interstellar communication. Any already 'communicable' extraterrestrial society we succeed in contacting soon would very likely be far ahead of us in these respects. The resultant information exchanges are surely going to be to our advantage rather than theirs; if they are willing to play along with us, it will not be because they expect to learn much of basic scientific and techno-logical value from Earth, but because they are curious about our understanding of these things and, perhaps, anxious to help us out for quite other reasons. I shall come to these 'other reasons' in a moment.

In the meantime, note just how beneficial contact with extra-terrestrials could be to us under these circumstances. Take the basic physical sciences first. There is no problem about their knowledge of these things being applicable to our own environment. They will certainly have the same mathematical tools we have: except that theirs will be more refined. The universe displays a common physics and inorganic chemistry; and as we say is likely to have a similar biochemistry. They will have known about relativity and photosynthesis and antimatter centuries, perhaps millenniums, before us. If we reflect on how much our knowledge has grown in the past century, and how much we expect it to grow within the next several decades, it becomes obvious that interstellar communication affords a marvellous opportunity to advance much faster than we could by our own efforts. Suppose we made up a list of problems our physicists, chemists, and mathematicians do not expect to solve for centuries and beam it to them for help. In reply they might transmit the complete proceedings of their most recent scientific symposia, with extensive footnotes explaining what led up to these results. In this way we could catch up with them, or almost so, in relatively short order, and then make a common assault on remaining problems. The same holds true for technology: though here the advantages are even more immediate and obvious. All technology is grounded in physics and chemistry, and should have, in principle at least, universal applicability. True, where there are significant variations in the basic elements prevalent, the composition of the atmosphere, or the force of gravity on the planetary surface, what we learn from extraterrestrials would have to be adapted to terrestrial conditions. Still these variations are not, as we saw, likely to be very great, and engineering principles would be identical. To see what kind of advances in technology we might hope for, consider how we might have benefited from being simply *informed* about rocket propulsion, transistors, and electron microscopes fifty years ago. Their knowledge of the descriptive sciences on the other hand, such as zoology, botany, ecology, geology, and geography, would have considerable interest to us, but of course less immediate usefulness. Similarly with the social sciences and the arts, which are of uncertain relevance to our own experience, though undoubtedly full of intrinsic interest on both sides.

I return now to the problem of motives prompting extra-terrestrials to engage in interstellar communication with us. For as we saw it is highly likely they will be more advanced scientifically and technologically than we. Upon receiving an answering signal from us, and then a continuous flow of information signals which reveals our current state of knowledge, they will quickly realise how relatively retarded we are compared to them. Far from directly benefiting by further exchange, they would know continued transmission on their side is a costly and – so far as scientific and technological knowledge is concerned – unre-warding undertaking. One is tempted to imagine them sending out just one brusque signal: 'Call us back a few millenniums from now, when you might prove more interesting.' However, that seems highly unlikely. A civilisation able to afford the enormous effort interstellar communication requires can hardly be motivated solely by practical considerations. They would want to know a lot about us and our planetary conditions: things that might even outweigh in importance, if they are really very advanced, further gains in scientific or technological knowledge. But would there not be still other reasons? Such a society, I suggested, would have a similar set of moral and legal concepts, arising from 'natural necessities' likely to apply just as much to its members as to members of the human community. It is in that context that feelings of fellowship, sympathy, concern, and even love for other persons arise. One does not have to suppose extraterrestrials 'more advanced' morally than we, or basically more altruistic than men normally are, to credit them with such motives. The 'moral neutrality' of the person-concept does not exclude, either, such feelings being attributed to extra-human persons. I should imagine, perhaps too generously, that such people would have towards a less advanced society of intelligent organisms the kind of 'impersonal' regard for their welfare many humans at present have towards less fortunate segments of their own race: or even, vaguely, towards their race as a whole. Underlying even this, I suppose, is the contingent fact that all such beings would have developed in a social situation where speech was learned during a long period of parental dependence. But whatever the root cause, these feelings do exist among human persons, and may be expected to appear among any people with similar evolutionary antecedents.

The question I set myself a little earlier can now be answered. Even between communities of intelligent organisms separated by such great distances that they have no reasonable expectation of physical confrontation and assimilation into a single society some sort of moral relations can be envisaged. True, it would make no sense to talk of 'mutual forbearances' in such a situation. However prone to bodily attack one society might be, the other will be invulnerable by virtue of that physical remoteness. For if interstellar travel between the two planetary sites is effectively ruled out, so is *sending objects* from one to the other. It would be hardly less difficult, technically speaking, to send a 1000-megaton thermonuclear missile across 50 light years of space than to send a spaceship that far. Nevertheless a kind of moral relation would obtain. For to engage in interstellar communication is, especially for the more advanced civilisation providing useful knowledge to the other, already to show a moral attitude. It is not *necessary* to do this: as we saw above, it is perfectly possible to be selfish about the whole thing. Where there are moral alternatives there is moral decision, and this involves treating the other community as a collective moral object. In Chapter 1 I argued that in addition to being a conceptualising entity the moral agent must be capable of experiencing sensations, emotions, feelings. Now it is true that an extraterrestrial community's relations with humans in the situation I am describing excludes causing physical pain or damage to each other (which reminds one of the argument in Chapter 2 against true machines having the status of persons or moral agents). However it does not exclude the causing of emotional stress or comfort. Suppose, for example, that after centuries of receiving helpful advice from an advanced extra-terrestrial civilisation they report the probable occurrence of a terrible catastrophe in the near future. They say a slow but irreversible malignant disease has broken out, or that a comet is heading unmistakably in their direction, and that by the time they get our next signal the end will be upon them. It could conceivably make some difference to them whether our last signal read: 'We're glad you smug know-it-alls are getting what you deserve'; or alternatively: 'We shall preserve your memory with gratitude and love.' And it could make some difference to our own moral stature, I suggest, which of these signals we sent. So that clearly, even where physical realities exclude the possibility of forming a viable society between humans and extraterrestrial persons, the notion of moral relations between them – attenuated and 'impersonal' as these would be – is still coherent and meaningful.

I come now to the third and final situation. In this situation we have *not* succeeded in establishing electromagnetic contacts with an extraterrestrial community, even after all the draconian efforts pictured at the end of Chapter 3. Yet at the same time our scientific 'substructure' for belief in the existence of intelligent extraterrestrial life has been greatly strengthened by further advances in biochemistry and astrophysics. Thus we conclude that advanced technological communities are rare in our galactic vicinity, perhaps far more than 1000 light years apart from each other, and that barring accidents and unforeseen developments we shall probably never communicate with one.

My question now becomes this: under such circumstances, where no moral relations are possible because of permanent physical separation, would continued belief in the existence of naturally evolved extra-human persons have any moral effect on the human community? Obviously it would not, at least in any direct way. One is reminded here of the situation described in my discussion of Hick's 'resurrection world' at the end of Chapter 1, since as I argued there no direct moral relations between the occupants of that abode and the living would be possible. However, there is a great difference. Humans who believe in an after-life of this sort expect to actually rejoin individual persons there, and this can affect their moral conduct. Belief in the existence of extraterrestrial persons is confined to the life we know in this world; it leads to no transcendent expectations at all, at least when held purely on the basis of scientific evidence, and the objects of the belief are not particular persons one has actually known. Still there is an indirect way in which it could affect us morally. What I mean is that it could comfort us to know, or have some scientific foundation for believing, that there are other natural persons in the universe somewhat like us physically, organised into moral communities, and sharing some of our own values. The search for knowledge, the desire for truth, the willingness to subordinate individual interest to social aims for the common benefit: these are all values without which no community of intelligent organisms could achieve a technological civilisation. If we are convinced such societies exist, though too distant for us to confirm our belief, we may have confidence some of our values will outlast our civilisation. Not that this would make them permanent: life itself is a transitory phenomenon in the history of the cosmos. But at least it could lay to rest the provincial humanist dogma that if we abandon belief in the Divine we have nothing to fall back on but Man's values. What we have to fall back on are the values, one may reasonably hold, of a potentially universal community of persons from which we are detached by the accidental dispersion of matter in the cosmos. That is pallid comfort, yet comfort of a kind.

Only one major question remains to be answered in this book. Leaving aside the possibility of artificial persons, which as I said before could exist at present only if naturally evolved extraterrestrial persons had already constructed them, we want to consider now if any persons other than natural persons could or in fact do exist. So at last we come to the issue of divine persons, the subject of the next and final chapter.

1. See R.N.Bracewell, 'Life in the Galaxy', reprinted in *Interstellar Communication*, ed. Cameron, as chapter 24, pp. 234–5.

2. See Macvey, *Journey to Alpha Centauri*, p. 146.

3. See Ehrensvärd, *Man on Another World*, ch. 4.

4. See H.C.Urey, 'The Origin of Organic Molecules', in *The Nature of Biological Diversity*, ed. by J.M.Allen (McGraw-Hill, 1963) pp. 1–13.

5. Cf. S.W.P.Steen in his review of Hans Freudenthal's *Lincos: Design of a Language for Cosmic Intercourse*, part 1, in *British Journal for the Philosophy of Science*, XII (1962) 336.

6. Cf. Bracewell, op. cit. p. 237.

7. See N.J.Berrill, *Worlds Without End*, chapters 9 and 10; Fred Hoyle, *Of Men and Galaxies* (University of Washington Press, 1964) ch. 2; and Robert Bieri, 'Huminoids on Other Planets?', in *American Scientist*, LII (1964).

8. Cf. Bieri, op. cit. pp. 453–7 especially.

9. See Hoyle, op. cit. p. 39. (Rather, sounds associated with speech are.)

10. Ibid.

11. Cf. Berrill, op. cit. p. 146.

12. Ibid. pp. 144–5.

13. Cf. ibid. p. 456.

14. Cf. ibid. p. 133.

15. Cf. Bieri, op. cit. p. 456.

16. Ibid.

17. See H.F.Blum, 'On the Origin and Evolution of Living Machines', in *American Scientist*, XLIX (1961); G.W.Beadle, *The Place of Genetics in Modern Biology* (1959); and especially G.G.Simpson, *This View of Life* (Harcourt and Longmans, 1964) ch. 13.

18. See I.S.Shklovskiy, 'Is Communication Possible with Intelligent Beings on Other Planets?', in *Interstellar Communication*, ed. Cameron, p. 11; Phillip Morrison, in *Interstellar Communication*, p. 236; and N.J.Berrill, op. cit. pp. 101 and 105.

19. See the report by J.P.T.Pearman in *Interstellar Communication*, ed. Cameron, chapter 28.

20. Cf. Sebastian van Hoerner, 'The Search for Signals from Other Civilizations', reprinted in *Interstellar Communication*, ed. Cameron, as chapter 27, p. 277; Hoyle, op. cit. p. 72; and Cameron, in *Interstellar Communication*, Introduction, p. 1.

21. See *The Concept of Law* (Clarendon Press, Oxford and N.Y., 1961) ch. 9, especially pp. 189–95.

5 Divine Persons

WE have already noted that in the past couple of decades there has emerged a scientific basis for belief in the existence of extraterrestrial natural persons. Now I take it as a serious matter that this belief does not constitute a vital part of the teachings of a single major terrestrial religion.

It is true some religions make allusions to extraterrestrials, or at least seem to, in their sacred writings and recorded revelations. There are hints of this, as mentioned earlier, in certain canonical documents of the Jain religion. When the founder, Mahavira, is proclaimed by Hindu gods, they invoke him to: 'Propagate the religion which is a blessing to all creatures in the world';[1] and farther on to: 'Establish the religion of the law which benefits all living beings in the universe.'[2] However, the systematic formulations of Jainist thought I have seen carry no reference to such beings.[3] Similarly with Buddhism. The treatise known as the *Saddharma-Pundarika*, or *The Lotus of the True Law*, depicts Bodhisattvas 'spread in all directions in hundred thousands of worlds',[4] yet apart from popular expressions of the religion this cosmic plenitude of Buddhas-to-be does not seem to play a significant role in the faith at all. Hinduism, for all its doctrinal tolerance and splendid mythological imagery, contains not a single reference to extraterrestrial intelligent organisms. Nor, to the best of my knowledge, does Sikhism, Zoroastrianism, or Islam: and, of course, not Confucianism, Taoism, or Shinto. Judaism contains one equivocal reference, a passage in the Hebrew commentary on Genesis called the *Midrash Rabba*, where the Holy One is said to be such that He 'builds worlds and destroys them'.[5]

Against this must be set the text of Genesis itself, where nothing of the kind is clearly implied: quite the contrary. And finally, of all the Christian sects only one – leaving aside Rosicrucianism, which is not a religion anyway – has had a 'revelation' relevant to this belief. That is the revelation of Joseph Smith the Prophet to his fellow Mormons in 1830, where he says that in his vision of Moses the latter 'beheld many lands; and each land was called earth, and there were inhabitants on the face thereof'.[6]

I cannot maintain, of course, that the above is an exhaustive account of the subject. Undoubtedly, when we first contact intelligent extraterrestrials, if we ever do, searching for further references to them in sacred writings will become a major preoccupation of religionists. But I do feel safe in saying not much more will be added to this list that is beyond scholarly dispute, and that in any case my generalisation about the relatively insignificant place of this belief in terrestrial religions holds true.

One might now ask why this should be a serious matter. Undoubtedly it is a far less serious matter to many of the Oriental faiths cited above, since in their 'higher' forms at least they teach salvation through individual enlightenment and conceive the supreme Reality in strictly impersonal terms.[7] The situation is quite different with the great monotheistic traditions, where salvation always involves a personal relationship between Creator and creatures, and where the supreme object of worship is still a Person. In such faiths God and humanity – along with subsidiary spiritual persons such as angels and jinns – constitute as it were a kingdom of moral beings: the sole objects of ultimate moral value in existence. One might fairly suppose, then, that to adherents of these religions the existence of extra-human natural persons in the universe would be an important item of religious knowledge. But before I go on to show why this should be the case, let us consider what can be said against any attempt to make scientific advances the basis for claims of revelational inadequacies in ancient faiths.

One of the most interesting defences I have seen against this sort of charge is Ninian Smart's discussion of the 'uncertainty principle' in religious belief.[8] He begins by admitting things look bad. There are many problems which make apologetics a difficult business: and among these are scientific discoveries one cannot reconcile with literal readings of the Bible. But what is the alternative? Is it conceivable that God should have produced a genuinely fundamentalistic Bible? Smart has no difficulty parodying such an expectation. The ultimate form of fundamentalism, he says, would be an arrangement of the stars so that they spell out the opening chapter of St John's Gospel; or the sprouting of Bibles from the soil like vegetables. But this is absurd. It is not that we would lose our freedom to worship God that way so much as the consideration that God is of necessity mysterious, hence could not be expected to reveal Himself so straightforwardly. Furthermore, a fundamentalist Bible implies that revelational truths about God can be learned parrot-wise. One cannot do that any more than one can learn science by mastering the body of knowledge in which science issues. This is why, Smart argues, it is out of place to expect God to have revealed to us modern scientific discoveries such as evolutionary theory and relativity physics: things we are better off learning for ourselves. God chose to intervene in human history at a time and a place where the only ideas about biology and cosmology understandable to men must necessarily appear – so Smart seems to be saying – out of date and obscurantist from a twentieth-century viewpoint. But that is just an entailment of Christianity's essential 'historicity', and it is profitless to speculate on superior dates and places for God's intervention.

I have stressed only those points in Smart's defence which bear directly on the topic I have in mind, but even this brief summary reveals, I think, a profound mistake. For if the Christian religion were in some sense 'true' – and this holds for Judaism and Islam as well – it is by no means clear that its 'historicity' precludes the revelation of factual matters beyond the scientific understanding

of men in ancient Palestine. No doubt God would have little
reason to 'reveal' relativity physics to them: this has no obvious
religious relevance, and probably couldn't be grasped without
nineteenth-century physics and mathematics anyway. Both the
Copernican picture of the solar system and the fact of human
evolution, on the other hand, certainly could have been understood, since Greek science advanced these hypotheses several
centuries before Christ. They do not seem of much religious
importance, I admit, and no doubt Christianity can be rendered
consistent with them by overlooking what the Bible actually says.
Nevertheless God did 'reveal' a contrary account of the movement
of heavenly bodies and of human origins, presumably knowing
His creatures would some day discover this is not the case.
Smart's pat explanation of this leaves one with the notion of a
peculiarly condescending deity, like a parent who encourages his
children to believe in Father Christmas.

To get back to my main point now, what about the existence
of extraterrestrial natural persons? It is no argument to say men of
the ancient Near East did not have sufficient understanding of
biochemistry and astrophysics to grasp the meaning of this
assertion. As remarked in Chapter 3, the Atomists envisaged it,
and so, apparently, did the authors of certain sacred writings in
Oriental religions. It is not necessary to knowledge that it be
gained *scientifically*, and of course no essential so-called religious
knowledge is ever gained that way. One can very well imagine
God saying to Moses, somewhat as Joseph Smith reported in his
vision: 'And I say unto thee, of every two score stars in the sky
one is a Sun like your own; and of these many are they with
planets like this very Earth; and on their surfaces are beings like
men, fallen and disgraced in mine eyes, but before whom the
path of righteousness lies open as to you; so that verily, my
servant, myriads are the worlds and legions beyond number the
beings I have created . . .' Why, then, do we find no mention of
this whatever in the basic scriptures of the great monotheistic

faiths? Why have the adherents to these faiths been allowed to think down through the ages that a drama involving only God and *Homo sapiens* was being played out on the cosmic stage? In this regard terrestrial monotheism seems just as provincial as humanism.

The only way around this criticism, it seems, is to deny that the existence of extraterrestrials really has religious significance. To see how hollow such a defence would be we need merely to remind ourselves of the discussion of person-artifacts at the end of Chapter 2. There I pointed out that we could have an artificially constructed species of intelligent and sentient organisms, on biological parity with *Homo sapiens*, yet distinct from it. After the first generation all descendants are naturally evolved, just as we are: the analogy with extraterrestrial organisms becomes particularly sharp here. Now the question arises how any monotheistic religion could be universal if these beings were not also capable of salvation in God's eyes? With regard especially to naturally evolved extraterrestrials, would they not have the same creaturely relation to Him as men have? Would they not stand in a moral relationship to God, just as men do? Would we not have exactly the same reasons for attributing souls to them as we have in the case of humans? What conceivable difference could it make that they should have, say, seven fingers on each hand, green skins, stunted bodies, or three rather than two pairs of appendages? They would be extra-human persons, but still persons. Any monotheistic system of religious beliefs which excludes extra-human natural persons from its scheme of salvation must display incredible theological partiality.

Let us be clear about what has been argued so far. I certainly have not shown that if extraterrestrial persons exist God was obliged to reveal this to us, so that the absence of such a revelation disproves the truth of our monotheistic traditions. Nevertheless I am saying the prospect of extraterrestrial intelligence, concerning which the principal sacred writings of Christianity, Judaism, and

Islam are absolutely silent, generates a profound suspicion that these terrestrial faiths are no more than that.

But in fact the situation is graver than this suggests. I said before that some Oriental religions are less affected by the absence, or at least sparsity, of allusions to extraterrestrial persons in their revelations, since salvation is achieved through individual illumination and union with an impersonal supreme Reality. Yet there is a further consideration, to which I turn now, that may be said to affect all terrestrial religions without distinction.

What I have in mind here arises from reflection on the very process of justification of any determinate system of religious beliefs. I begin by drawing attention to Alasdair MacIntyre's famous discussion of this problem in section 5 of his essay, 'The Logical Status of Religious Belief'.[9] MacIntyre jettisons all attempts to construe religious beliefs as explanatory hypotheses about the existence and structure of the universe. Rather he sees the only possible justification of such beliefs in the acceptance of a particular authority. There may be no shared content in the great religions, he says, but each has its own procedure for deciding whether a given belief or practice is or is not authentic, its criterion by means of which orthodoxy is determined. That authority is determined by the body of religious tradition as we find it. Just as in locating the source of sovereignty in a political body, there is no *external* justification possible. The acceptance or rejection of a religion thus reduces to the acceptance or rejection of such an authority. Authority is not itself worshipped, but it is accepted as defining the worshipful. Ultimately the only 'apologia' for a religion is to describe its content in detail. Then a man will either find himself brought to say 'My Lord and my God', or he will not.

Despite appearances, there are compensations for religionists in MacIntyre's reduction of justification to the acceptance of internal authority. For, by eschewing all appeals to external criteria as a means of justifying belief, the particular religious tradition –

assuming its central creeds coherent – is also secured against external criticism. This tallies with the emphasis MacIntyre and many contemporary theologians have put on the rootedness of religious beliefs in an attitude of worship. One is invited, so to speak, to enter the temple, look around, listen to the chants: and then one either wants to stay or one walks out. What we cannot properly do is to stand outside and form an 'objective' judgment of what is going on inside.

But the difficulty is that there is not, to pursue this illustration, just one temple. There are at least a dozen large and old ones, with lots of smaller and some new ones scattered about. It's all very well to justify being in *a* temple this way, rather than outside it. But how does one justify being in *that* temple rather than another? One can always say: 'Because this is the one whose authority I accept.' Unfortunately that is like saying one married 'the only girl in the world for me', when in fact she was the only girl one ever got to know well. In the overwhelming majority of cases people in particular temples never had occasion, at least in their religiously formative years, to enter other temples and become familiar with their contents. Indeed most religious believers are not even aware of the existence of more than a few rival temples. Apart from a disposition to adopt a worshipful attitude, the only explanation – not justification – for accepting a particular religious authority in all but an insignificant number of cases is the accident of birth and early environment. One enters *that* temple, if any, because one's parents or community worship there. And yet, as MacIntyre admits, the great religions have no shared content. They tend irrevocably to exclude each other. If one is true, all the others must, in doctrinal matters at least, be false. Otherwise they are saying nothing about the world at all, hypothetically or not.

Assuming that human religions do make factual claims, even if these are not held as provisional hypotheses, it ought to be extremely important which, if any, of these religions is true. The difficulty developed above is that one could not know that, because holding a system of religious beliefs to be true involves no more than accepting the authority found within that religious tradition. I want now to broaden our context somewhat by returning to the subject of extraterrestrial persons. As we saw in previous chapters there are good grounds for supposing communities of such beings to exist throughout the universe, however distant from each other they may be. *Qua* moral agents, there seems no reason to doubt they would have developed religious traditions of their own. But if so, does that not imply an enormous number of 'temples' available to intelligent beings in the cosmos? For there may well be, as we saw in Chapter 3, one hundred million sites of extraterrestrial intelligence in our galaxy alone, and there are at least 10^{10} galaxies in the universe. If each such community had only one distinct religion of its own that would yield 10^{18} independent religious traditions, each making truth-claims the ultimate justification for which amounts to acceptance of an authority within that particular religious tradition.

This prospect must be so staggering to the human religionist that every effort will be made, I am sure, to subvert it. The easiest way to do that, of course, is simply to deny the existence of extra-human persons. But since that has the dangerous implication of making terrestrial faiths falsifiable, another and seemingly sounder course would be to argue that extraterrestrial religions need not be 'independent' of our own at all. For surely if, as I myself maintained in Chapter 4, extra-human persons are so much like us, we could in principle form a moral community with them, then we could also form with them – again in principle – a single religious community. And indeed that is just what adherents to 'universal' human religions will want to insist is the case. If all humans could be Christians or Moslems or Buddhists, why could not all intelligent organisms be so?

Here we must be very careful to separate two questions easily lumped together. The first is whether it is possible in principle that some main features of a given terrestrial religion should occur – perhaps by divine intervention – in extraterrestrial communities as well, so that in this limited sense at least there could be a truly universal religion. I do not see how anyone could deny that possibility undogmatically. The second is whether it is likely that in fact a given terrestrial religious *tradition* should have its counterpart in extraterrestrial communities. This is quite another matter indeed, as I shall now endeavour to show.

In his book *World Religions* Professor Smart makes an insightful remark. A representative of Christianity under attack for what he calls 'the scandal of particularity', i.e. the specific historicity of the Incarnation (I shall have more to say about that later), replies to his non-Christian opponents as follows: 'I can't help but feel that wherever a religion goes back to a historical teacher (and Buddhism does) or to a certain historical tradition (and surely Hinduism looks back to the Veda), you're bound to get particularism. Now all the great religions are in some way or other traditional; so that we're all equally implicated in this scandal.'[10] Of course the others protest, quite rightly, that their religions are not implicated to the *same extent* as Christianity, but they do not deny being so implicated.

That some terrestrial faiths are 'particularistic' to a degree that they are entirely unsuitable as truly universal religions will hardly be questioned. According to Shinto sacred scriptures, for example, the first divine creation was the islands of Japan, the first Mikado was a descendant to Earth from the Sun-Goddess Amaterasu; and until quite recently the Emperor of Japan was revered as an incarnate divine being. Unless one wants to suppose there are Japanese extraterrestrials, I need say no more. But since in fact all the major terrestrial religions trace their authority back to a particular human teacher or prophet, or humanly composed recording document, the difference in their 'particularism' can only be a matter of degree. They will inevitably take on all sorts of particularistic accretions, inseparable from the central beliefs of the faith in so far as it is a living religious tradition, which could by no stretch of the imagination be duplicated or multiplicated elsewhere.

Consider that most varied and accommodating religious tradition we call Hinduism. Undoubtedly the Upanishads give us an exalted conception of a higher Reality, but who is to say *this* is Hinduism? The earliest Vedas indicate a kind of nature-worship not unlike the Shinto religion, except that the primeval person's bodily organs (human in structure, of course) become the sources of four social castes. Even as late as the *Bhagavad Gita* the new incarnate deity Krishna is declared to have said *he* created the castes. The idea of immutable hereditary social structures seems in fact the only feature of Hinduism present throughout all its historical phases and scriptural recordings. Are we to seriously envisage all communities of extraterrestrial persons divided into four hereditary castes: a system which never extended itself beyond the Indian subcontinent on our own Earth, throughout several millenniums? Or take the apparently trivial abstention from eating beef and the corresponding regard for sacred cows. Undoubtedly extraterrestrials would have domesticated animals of some kind, but what they almost certainly would not have are cows. The chances of this animal being reproduced elsewhere are on a par with the chances of extraterrestrials being 'human' in the biological sense. So how could this item of popular Hinduism occur in other planetary systems? There must be whole tracts of Hindu beliefs that cannot have relevance to the socio-historical experience and planetary environment of extraterrestrial organisms. Yet they are composites of the living religious tradition.

I despair of trying to examine all the major religious traditions exhaustively from this point of view, but a few generalisations about some may clear the way for a closer look at others. Confucianism and Taoism are so deeply immersed in a specifically Chinese culture that it is difficult to imagine them functioning as religious traditions anywhere else. The former is almost completely bound up with social, political, and familial duties; the latter, while emphasising a mystical 'way' to union with the Supreme Being, nevertheless embraces in its popular forms all kinds of Chinese superstitions. This is noted not in a spirit of criticism, by the way, but in order to urge the unlikelihood of such religions having universal applicability. Even more striking is the fact that whatever may have been their intentions, the founders of both these religions were subsequently venerated by their followers. For about 1200 years Confucius was worshipped in the temples: as late as 1906 he was considered 'Co-assessor with the deities Heaven and Earth'.[11] As early as A.D. 156, on the other hand, Lao-Tse was the object of state sacrifices; by the fourth century he was believed to have had a supernatural origin; and subsequently he was in fact apotheosised as a member of the Taoist Trinity.[12] Much the same is true, I am afraid, of Jainism and Sikhism. Though both began as reform movements within India – Jainism very long ago and Sikhism comparatively recently – neither succeeded in freeing itself entirely from the particularistic shell of Hinduism. Jainism, for example, now has the caste system, and Sikhs retain the doctrines of Karma, the transmigration of souls, etc. Again an even more striking feature is apotheosis of the founder, quite apart from his original teachings. Mahavira is pictured as sinless, omniscient, and an incarnate deity;[13] the Guru Nanak was revered during the latter part of his life as a saint and even divine saviour: within sixty years of his death he was considered the Supreme God, or Brahma, himself.[14]

This rather characteristic development in many living religions deserves a special emphasis. For we must recognise that a religious tradition is not merely what the founder taught or the original canonical documents say. It is everything that it has become up to the present: that is one of the reasons why contemporary philosophers of religion insist upon understanding typical theological utterances in the whole context of liturgy and worship. So that when in fact the overwhelming majority of adherents to a given faith come to apotheosise its founder, as in the cases above, there is no point in just overriding this as a 'corruption of the true belief'. Authority, to paraphrase MacIntyre again, is determined by the body of religious tradition as we find it. And, if so, that presents a particular difficulty against the background of extraterrestrial religious communities, differing only in degree from the problem of universalising a narrow national faith such as Shinto. For whatever *else* they became in the eyes of their followers, Confucius and Lao-Tse, Mahavira and Nanak were certainly human beings. In most cases we know, indeed, a great deal about them: their origins (e.g. their 'human' parents, social backgrounds), their early lives, consecrations to the religious way of life, ministries, struggles, and even deaths. To share in the religious traditions they founded would require extraterrestrials to worship an individual human being (or if you like, divine person in human form) who did this or that and taught this or that on the surface of our planet around one sun in one galaxy. Nor will it do to say the deified founder could have 'taken on' extraterrestrial fleshly form elsewhere. He could hardly be expected to live the same *life* among non-humans; and he would certainly not be the same *person* (I shall develop this point later on, in the more complex case of Christianity). Thus it is grossly improbable that the same religious tradition, if ever it apotheosised any human being, should be shared by extraterrestrials.

It is not always realised to what an extent the same fatal handicap has developed among still other ancient living faiths. Zoroastrianism, for instance, began as a purely monotheist (or dualistic monotheist) religion. Indeed it is the oldest major surviving faith to have had universalist aspirations involving the voluntary conversion of mankind (though over the past four centuries it has lapsed into the hereditary religion of the Parsi community). In later sacred documents, however, Zoroaster is depicted as pre-existent 3000 years before his 'physical birth', until then resident with and equal to the archangels; as having had a virgin birth; and as deserving of worship along with the deity Ahura Mazda.[15] Apparently the last three saviours of the world will be supernatural descendants from Zoroaster himself.[16] Thus one cannot adhere to this religious tradition today without identifying it integrally with a single human being and his mission on Earth.

Much the same can be said, surprisingly, of Buddhism: in spite of its already noted allusions to the possible plurality of Buddhas. In the 'Greater Vehicle', or Mahayana tradition, which stresses the Bodhisattva doctrine, the Lord Buddha is in fact viewed as an incarnate god: supernaturally conceived, miraculously born, sinless, omniscient, everlasting.[17] But even so there can be little doubt who Buddha was. We know much of his life on our planet, and there is no human person whose image has found such numerous representations in idol form. Again we could hardly expect 'other' Buddhas in other worlds to have lived the same life or to have appeared in the same body, yet surely it must be the same *person* if the same religious tradition is shared by extra-terrestrials. Of course this criticism will not apply to the 'Lesser Vehicle', or Theravada tradition. The latter shuns theological speculation entirely, and contents itself with the *arhat* ideal of attaining Nirvana by individual liberating contemplation, or Enlightenment. But for the same reasons there is no unifying religious principle in Theravadin Buddhism: one can fairly say it is an 'agnostic' faith,[18] or more properly, a way of personal salvation independent of any ultimate assertions about the world. Nevertheless, even here he who 'showed the way' is a particular human person. Extraterrestrial Thervadins would not have had the same teacher or share the same religious tradition.

There remain to be considered now those major terrestrial religions which form a continuous historical 'family': Judaism, Islam, and Christianity. With regard to the parent religious tradition, Judaism, I don't suppose anyone will doubt its particularistic character. To be a Jew even today requires identification with the history of a particular segment of the human race: their exodus from Egypt, their acceptance of the Ten Commandments through Moses, their settlement in Palestine, their kings and wars and prophets and exile and sacred literature and rituals and laws. No doubt there could be similar segments of extraterrestrial races 'chosen' by God to set an example to the rest. What there could not be is an identical religious tradition elsewhere. Suppose we make contact with an extraterrestrial civilisation and send them, *inter alia*, the complete text of the Torah. Could anyone reasonably expect that, after translation, a segment of that race would be able to recognise this as describing not only their cosmological and theological beliefs, but also their history as a people or nation? Yet, as I said, the history of the Jewish people is an integral part of the Judaic religious tradition.

Islam, at least at first sight, is in a very different situation. Though it had – as any religion does – its origins among a particular people at a certain time and place, Islam was from its inception 'universal' in outlook. The very meaning of its title, 'submission to God', bespeaks the widest possible applicability; and there has never been any claim that its human founder, Muhammad, was more than the last true prophet whose prophecy abrogates all others. Also, though the Koran consists of Muhammad's sayings in Arabic as recorded by his followers, the faithful regard these as God's revelation *through* Muhammad, who was thus only His 'Messenger' on Earth. Nothing in these central features of the religion, then, rules out its duplication or multiplication among extraterrestrial communities. However, it is not the central tenets of a faith, I have been insisting all along, which constitute a religious *tradition*. When we turn to some of the detailed contents of that religious tradition we find all sorts of particularistic accretions that could hardly have their analogues among extraterrestrials. Without being frivolous, could we expect extra-human peoples to direct their prayers towards Mecca; to make pilgrimages there from their planetary *loci*; to observe the Ramadhan fast in the absence of a Moon; to abstain from eating pork when there are no pigs to eat; and so on? No doubt there could be a religion *like* Islam elsewhere, but many of the koranic commandments and injunctions would be so utterly inapplicable to them that the respective religious traditions would have little shared content, and the source of authority in each would necessarily be distinct from the others. But I need belabour this point no further.

We may now turn to a consideration of Christianity in this context. Thinking Christians confess, as I noted earlier, to a greater implication in the 'scandal of particularity' than any other major living religious tradition. For almost from its inception Christians regarded the founder of their faith as God incarnate: not, as in other faiths, because of subsequent veneration, but immediately upon his last appearance to them. Nor, for that matter, was Jesus of Nazareth apotheosised independently from or even in spite of his own teachings; and in contrast to many other living religions, there is no room in Christianity for a succession of other incarnations or enlightened teachers on Earth sharing in the founder's cosmic status. On all these grounds, not to mention others, Christianity is easily the most particularistic terrestrial faith of importance or influence to also have universalist aspirations.

The familiar complaint of non-Christians to all this is that, since Jesus' history is very particular indeed, most of humanity has been excluded from direct salvation by never having had an opportunity to hear the 'good news' of Christ's coming and teachings. But of course the situation becomes far worse against the background of universal biochemical evolution. For if the Gospel were spread only on this planet none but an insignificant fraction of intelligent organisms would have heard it. Professor Milne's suggestion a decade and a half ago that we might succeed in spreading the Gospel to other beings in the galaxy through radiocommunication, and that they would then spread it to local galaxies, and they to 'the whole intergalactic universe',[19] can hardly be taken seriously. It would require almost one hundred thousand years for a radiowave to reach the farthest star in our own galaxy, and about two million years to reach the nearest other galaxy. As we saw in Chapter 3, the farthest known galaxies, constituting probably only one-tenth the total intergalactic universe, are receding from us so rapidly that everything beyond them would be entirely inaccessible to us: even if we did not have to spread this message *via* ten thousand million intervening galaxies. Thus there is absolutely no hope of the Christian religion becoming known to all extra-human persons in the universe if, in fact, the Earth is its sole point of origin.

Perhaps in recognition of this difficulty, Professor Mascall subsequently rejected the Milne Plan for universal salvation in favour of another which does not assume the uniqueness of Christ on our own planet.[20] Mascall begins by denying that knowledge of the Incarnation is strictly necessary for salvation. The attitude of the great classical tradition of Christian thought, he says, finds the essence of redemption in the fact that the Son of God has hypostatically united to Himself the nature of the species He came to redeem. The Son of God became man in order that, in Him, men might become the sons of God. One need not recoil in horror at the prospect of countless incarnations and crucifixions in the universe. If this were necessary, the fact that it ended, through Christ's resurrection, in the glory and victory of human redemption on this planet is enough to justify its occurrence everywhere else. Except on the extreme kenotic view – that between His Incarnation and Ascension the Son of God more or less lost His divine attributes and was temporarily nothing *but* man – Christianity has no conclusive theological reasons for opposing multiple incarnations in which non-human rational corporeal beings would have their natures hypostatically united to that of the same Son of God. If no change in the Godhead is involved in the Incarnation on Earth, if the Incarnation takes place not by the conversion of the Godhead into flesh, but by the taking up of manhood into God, then why should not other finite rational creatures be united hypostatically to the Person of the Divine word? In other words, if finite and infinite natures are *once* compatible in the same Person, why not several times?

But in that case, one might ask, why not multiple incarnations on Earth itself, so that all segments of mankind should have heard the 'good news'? Mascall is very careful to separate these two questions. That Socrates or Gautama Buddha might, equally with Jesus of Nazareth, be incarnations of the divine Word he flatly rejects. The Word became man, he says, by assuming a particular human nature that 'had no personal individuality of its own', and in assuming it conferred His personal individuality upon it. If God conferred His personal individuality upon human nature twice over there would still be only one individual: which is just to say human nature could not in fact be assumed more than once, 'since it is individualised in his Person and that Person is numerically one'. Nothing would be achieved by a second incarnation that was not achieved by the first, which offered renewal and restoration to every member of the human race by incorporation into Christ's manhood. The very possibility of this incorporation, Mascall argues, turns on the fact that they are *men* and Christ is *man*, i.e. that He took upon Himself their nature. From this it will not follow in the least that non-human rational species can be incorporated into His *manhood*. Another redeemed species will be incorporated into Christ's X-hood, whatever that may be, by an incarnation of the divine Word in *their* nature.

Concerning this certainly impressive theological excursion I have just two points to urge. Either one or the other, I shall argue, *must* apply to the Mascallian scheme for a truly universal Christianity; and if I am right there is no way for the religion to escape both, short of risking something even more dangerous. I shall try to make this clear as I go along.

The first point arises from the consideration that a stricter monotheism would be open to Christianity, and perhaps a more flexible incarnation-concept, if we do not suppose God became man, but merely took on the *appearance* of man in Jesus of Nazareth. It would be a stricter monotheism because the unity of the Godhead would not be threatened by postulating three distinct Persons in one nature. It would be more flexible as an incarnation-concept because God could take the appearance of even an infinite number of natural persons in the universe. Also, of course, God could then appear many times within any rational corporeal species, as certain Oriental religions suppose has actually taken place.

Unfortunately for this alternative, it has already been condemned as heretical by Christian orthodoxy. It is no less than 'docetism', the view that Christ on Earth was not really of human flesh, but composed of some celestial substance, if not actually a phantasm. For better or worse, Christianity long ago decided against the docetists, on the grounds that if Christ is to be fully real He must have had full humanity.[21] But in that case it follows Jesus Christ was both a full human person and the Son of God, which leads into my second point.

Here I have to back up for a moment and remind readers of a claim I made in the first chapter of this book. I said there that P. F. Strawson's concept of a 'person' was too narrow because it arbitrarily excluded incorporeal persons: particularly God. Whether in fact God exists, either as a single Supreme Person or as three Persons sharing one substance (Christians talk both ways about God), is not my present concern at all. Nor am I concerned, really, with the puzzling question of how Jesus Christ could be both the Son of God and a fully real human person. What I am concerned with is this: that surely no single organic person can be more than *one* organic person, however many incorporeal persons he may be at the same time.

We are all familiar with the case of identical twins. Often these are so much alike, at least organically, that close relatives cannot

tell them apart. But to tell them apart and to know – if one knows
there are twins to begin with – that they are *two distinct persons* are
quite different matters. Here Mr Strawson's descriptive metaphysics is entirely apposite. They are not 'the same person' because
they can be identified and reidentified by referring to distinct
places at the same time. Now incorporeal persons may be
everywhere at any time. But corporeal persons can be in only one
place in the universe at the same time. The problem, then, is to
understand how the Son of God could have multiple incarnations
– perhaps as many as 10^{18} such incarnations – in the universe
without being simultaneously incarnate in more than one organic
person. Of course He could not. If one accepts the above figure
as probable sites of extraterrestrial natural person-communities
within the *known* galaxies (only about one-tenth of all galaxies);
and if one accepts Jesus of Nazareth's life-time as typical of
incarnations of the Son of God; then 34×10^{18} years would have
to pass for the Son of God to have gone from birth to resurrection
just once in succession on each such planet. But the future life-
spans of stars whose planetary systems are likely to permit the
evolution of intelligent organisms is only $(1-5) \times 10^{10}$ years in our
own galaxy; so that if this were also typical of the known intergalactic universe, there would be on the order of 680,000,000 to
3,400,000,000 incarnations occurring simultaneously from now to
the extinction of life on all such stars. Allowing for earlier
incarnations reduces this figure a bit, but not enough to make any
real difference.

I return now to my second point. If God did not merely take
the *appearance* of any individual member of a rational corporeal
species, but through His Son 'assumed their nature' in each case,
thereby conferring on this species 'His personal individuality', it
follows there were or are or will be multiple organic persons in the
universe who are 'divine persons' in the Christian sense *at the same
time*. What this implies for Christianity can be easily seen in the
following imaginative exercise. Suppose we contact another

civilisation 50 light years distant from us and beam to them the text of the New Testament. In reply they send us, say, a televised picture of *their* Christ. He has nine dactyls on each arm, four legs, a thick blue skin, and wispy, elongated bones. We could hardly radio back 'Yes, this is the Christ', unless we meant by that no more than 'This is how the Son of God *appeared* to you': sheer docetism again. But on the other hand we could not deny His divine status (assuming He preached a 'Sermon on the Mount', died on the cross for their sins, was resurrected, etc.), since He would have the same claims to this as Jesus of Nazareth. What are we to do then? We have Jesus Christ and they have 'X-Christ', both natures having been assumed by God and both species incorporated into Christ's 'manhood' and 'X-hood', respectively, as separate incarnations of the divine Word. Yet in each case the assumption of those natures is, in Mascall's words, 'individualised in his person and that Person is numerically one'. But if the Son of God is numerically one how can He also be fully human and fully 'X' at the same time, i.e. two distinct corporeal persons? For two corporeal persons are not one. What is more, we should then have just as much reason to worship the 'X-Christ' as to worship Jesus Christ, and Christianity would embrace no longer a Trinity but a Quaternity.[22]

The only way I can see for Christians to escape this dilemma is, as I warned above, to risk something far more dangerous to the faith than docetism on one side and conceptual collapse on the other. For what were once heretical views have sometimes become orthodoxy later; and only a small proportion of religious believers understand creedal implications well enough to be disturbed by mere incoherence. What Christianity can do is to turn its back, so to speak, on the whole prospect of extraterrestrial intelligence. And it can do this in two ways. First, it can flatly deny the existence of extra-human natural persons. But as I hinted earlier in a more general context, this has the unwelcome implication that Christianity is falsifiable. In fact it would mean that, perhaps alone among the major living religions, Christianity could be *proven* false by experiments in interstellar communication.[23] (As MacIntyre's analysis shows, it is very important to religious beliefs that they not be held hypothetically.) Second, Christianity can simply renounce all claims at being a truly universal religion, insist on the uniqueness of the terrestrial Incarnation, and accept the full implications of its excessive particularism.

If I may I should like to go back now to a related topic discussed rather inconclusively in Chapter 1. Near the end of that chapter I considered John Hick's account of personal survival as compared to P. F. Strawson's. I agreed that whereas disembodied survival is a very grim prospect – grimmer than Strawson's analysis allows – Hick's account overcomes these disadvantages by endowing deceased humans with a 'replica' body resident in a spatially distinct 'resurrection world'. I went on to point out that in spite of these improvements such persons would be totally cut off from the living human persons they left behind (until such time as those successors join them in that special abode), hence could not have any direct moral relations with them. As for the *truth* of Hick's picture, which was designed not only to make meaningful the notion of an after-life, but to show how Christian theism could find 'eschatological verification', some of the points made in the present chapter may allow us to reach a definite conclusion about that now.

One will note, first of all, that the Hickian scheme for survival requires each human person having *two* bodies. Not, of course, at the same time: which, as we have seen, is impossible. Rather the person in question leaves one body at the instant of death and, so to speak, finds himself in another immediately thereafter. This in itself is not without difficulties. For the ante-mortem body normally goes on existing, though dead and rotting, at the same time one takes on a post-mortem 'replica' body in the 'resurrection world'. At the very least this implies a dissociation of the person from his body which some very able contemporary philosophers, such as Antony Flew,[24] have made us realise is by no means easy to envisage. However, Hick goes out of his way to render this plausible by having deceased persons endowed with *similar* bodies in the resurrection world: the material is entirely different, but the shape is the same, and one has even the same memory traces as before. It is this feature, of course, that enables us to know who we are and to recognise other people in the 'resurrection world'.

Still Hick admits that finding oneself in this situation does not itself constitute a verification of Christian theism. The honest atheist might regard what has happened to him as merely a 'surprising natural fact', making the universe more complex and perhaps more to be approved of, but just as 'religiously ambiguous' as before. Hick devotes the rest of his essay[25] to showing how that ambiguity could be removed.

The most tempting way to do that would be to suppose every resurrected person will have a direct confrontation with God. But as Hick acknowledges, it is certainly difficult to imagine what that would be like in view of the absolute and abstract nature of God. Fortunately for Christian theism, the problem is overcome through the Incarnation. Quoting Barth, Hick says: 'Jesus Christ is the knowability of God.' In confronting Jesus a sense of the fulfilment of divine purpose for human life is apprehended *as* the fulfilment of that purpose. 'The presence of Christ in his Kingdom marks this as being beyond doubt the Kingdom of the God and Father of the Lord Jesus Christ.'

But *which* Christ? If there are extraterrestrial resurrected persons in this abode – and there certainly should be if extra-human natural persons exist – they are not going to recognise Jesus of Nazareth as their Christ. They will recognise Christ only as a person having a body like their own in shape or form. And if there are, say, 10^{18} species of resurrected persons, there would have to be 10^{18} Christs in the 'resurrection world': each slightly different from the others. But then we have the same problem we had with the ante-mortem universe. For each body of Christ is still an object occupying space (even in the distinct space of the 'resurrection world'), and no two Christs could, therefore, be the same. The most one can say for Hick's scheme is that it makes plausible – though only vaguely* – the verification of Christian theism *as a terrestrial faith*. On the postulate of there being extraterrestrial persons necessitating multiple incarnations, the existence of such a 'resurrection world' would indeed falsify orthodox Christianity's claims to the status of a truly universal religion.

It has sometimes been suggested by philosophical theists that, although the classic proofs of God's existence taken severally do not provide conclusive grounds for belief in God, each is a 'pointer' or 'indicator' of His existence and, taken together, they do amount to a reasonable presumption in favour of that belief. To this it has been replied, quite rightly, that a fallacious argument points nowhere and that no number of such arguments will make up for the inadequacy of each.[26] The same would hold, surely, for any number of attempted *dis*proofs of God's existence, where each fails to reach its mark. But all such proofs and disproofs proceed in a strictly deductive manner, however much empirical data may be included in one or more key premisses. What I have been trying to do in this chapter, building on what went before, is to show how a correct analysis of the person-concept combined with the not unreasonable belief in extraterrestrial natural persons actually undermines belief in God. There is still room here for a suitably abstract God-concept, but the vital links between such a concept and our religious traditions become strained to the breaking-point. For make no mistake about it, unless the Divine can be *both* integrally instrumental in our own lives and the Supreme Master of the universe, this concept loses all its force. How He could be the God of all intelligent organisms – whether in our present world

* I say 'vaguely' because Hick does not show how the resurrected atheist would recognise Jesus of Nazareth as the Christ. Most of his contemporaries in Palestine did not.

or a fancied 'resurrection world' – has been sufficiently questioned above. How, failing that, the existence of such an abstract Author of the universe would have any real religious importance to all the presumed communities of natural persons in His creation is extremely unclear. For my part, to acknowledge that sort of Supreme Person would make no difference whatever to a consistent religious atheism. In sum, we cannot have a vital religious tradition – hence necessarily particularistic – and at the same time a plausibly 'universal' system of religious beliefs. That is the true upshot of the Copernican Revolution in our time.

What we can do, of course, is to abandon all particularistic religious beliefs whatever. And if one says that would be tantamount to jettisoning not only the prospect of a universal religion but religion itself, I would agree. But not the religious *attitude*, or at least not entirely. For underlying the tendency of men to abase themselves before some imagined superior being there was always, I think, a striving for 'otherness': a moving away from one's individuality and even humanity towards something beyond them which could perhaps offer understanding, sympathy, love. No doubt this desire has its roots in childhood dependence, but it is a genuine need. If this book has a conclusion it is that in contemplating and possibly discovering the existence of extra-human natural persons we may find something to satisfy, in some measure, that striving. For it is in that direction, and not in the direction of sophisticated machines or theological abstractions, that a plausible 'otherness' lies. Thus the religious attitude, or an important element of it, may yet survive the death of all determinate religious beliefs.

1. *Sacred Books of the East*, ed. F. Max Müller (Oxford, 1879–1910) xx 195.

2. Ibid. xx 256.

3. Cf. Mohan Lal Mehta, *Outlines of Jaina Philosophy* (Jain Mission Society, Bangalore City, 1954); and Nathmal Fatia, *Studies in Jaina Philosophy* (Jain Cultural Research Society, Banares, 1951).

4. *Sacred Books of the East*, ed. Müller, xxi 365. Sullivan, in *We Are Not Alone*, p. 287, quotes from chapter 15 of this work. However, it is clear from the context (pp. 299–300) that the Lord Buddha was there making a spatial analogy to time, in order to show he has been the All-wise from eternity. Similar phraseology depicting the immensity of the populated universe is found in chapters 20 and 23.

5. Quoted in Sullivan, op. cit. p. 288.

6. Ibid. p. 287.

7. On both these points, see Ninian Smart, *World Religions: A Dialogue* (Pelican, 1966), especially chapters 4 and 6.

8. 'The Uncertainty Principle in Religion', in *The Listener*, LXVI 1961.

9. In *Metaphysical Beliefs*, ed. S. E. Toulmin (SCM Press, 1957). The section referred to is entitled 'The Justification of the Religious Attitude'.

10. Smart, *World Religions*, p. 97.

11. See R. E. Hume, *The World's Living Religions* (Scribner's, 1953 ed.) p. 115.

12. See Hume, op. cit. pp. 132–3.

13. See Hume, op. cit. pp. 46–7.

14. See Hume, op. cit. p. 92.

15. See Hume, op. cit. p. 199.

16. See Hume, op. cit. p. 210.

17. See Hume, op. cit. p. 67.

18. See Smart, *World Religions*, p. 62.

19. E. A. Milne, *Modern Cosmology and the Christian Idea of God* (Oxford, 1952) p. 153.

20. E. L. Mascall, *Christian Theology and Natural Science* (Archon and Longmans, 1956) pp. 38–42 especially.

21. Smart, op. cit. ch. 6.

22. See Smart, op. cit. p. 104, where he suggests the same.

23. See Smart, op. cit., for a similar concession.

24. Cf. his 'Can a Man Witness His Own Funeral?', in *Hibbert Journal* (1956); and 'Death', in *New Essays in Philosophical Theology*, ed. A. Flew and A. MacIntyre (SCM Press and Macmillan Co., N.Y., 1956) pp. 267–72.

25. In *The Existence of God*; see pp. 269–73.

26. See Alasdair MacIntyre, *Difficulties in Christian Belief* (SCM Press, 1959) p. 63.